J. F. KENNEDY

A BEGINNER'S GUIDE

PETER NEVILLE

Hodder & Stoughton

A MEMBER OF THE HODDER HEADLINE GROUP

Orders: please contact Bookpoint Ltd, 130 Milton Park, Abingdon, Oxon OX14 4SB. Telephone: (44) 01235 827720, Fax: (44) 01235 400454. Lines are open from 9.00–6.00, Monday to Saturday, with a 24-hour message answering service. Email address: orders@bookpoint.co.uk

British Library Cataloguing in Publication Data
A catalogue record for this title is available from The British Library

ISBN 0 340 84615 1

First published 2002
Impression number   10 9 8 7 6 5 4 3 2 1
Year 2007 2006 2005 2004 2003 2002

Cover photo from Corbis
Typeset by Transet Limited, Coventry, England.
Printed in Great Britain for Hodder & Stoughton Educational, a division of Hodder Headline Plc, 338 Euston Road, London NW1 3BH by Cox & Wyman, Reading, Berks.

J. F. KENNEDY

A BEGINNER'S GUIDE

CONTENTS

▬ ▬

DEDICATION

To my father

John Kennedy's Life and Times

John F. Kennedy was one of the most charismatic presidents in the history of the United States. Many people can remember where they were when the news came through that Kennedy had been shot in Dallas, Texas on 22 November 1963. Yet Kennedy was president for less than three years, and he failed to implement many of the reforms that he had promised during the 1960 election campaign. But despite this, the Kennedy Presidency has the whiff of **Camelot** about it, and in the face of recent disclosures about John Kennedy's private life, the romance endures.

Kennedy promised a **New Frontier**, and his premature death made many Americans feel cheated of the promise associated with him. Dead at only 46, Kennedy had come to epitomize youth, vitality, and charm.

THE UNITED STATES AT THE TIME OF JOHN KENNEDY

John Fitzgerald Kennedy was born on 29 May 1917 in Boston, Massachusetts, the descendant of Irish immigrants who had become prominent in local politics. His father Joseph P. Kennedy, was a very successful businessman (although some claimed that his fortune came from the illegal sale of alcohol in the **Prohibition** period), while his mother, Rose Fitzgerald, was the daughter of 'Honey Fitz', a colourful former Mayor of Boston.

KEYWORDS

Camelot: the court of the legendary King Arthur. The term was used in the USA to sum up the romantic, youthful promise of the Kennedy Presidency.

New Frontier: in his acceptance speech at the Democratic Convention in July 1960, Kennedy spoke of a 'New Frontier' where the United States could fulfil its destiny by removing 'all forms of human poverty.'

Prohibition: in 1919 the US Congress accepted the 18th amendment to the Constitution which prevented the manufacture, sale or transportation of alcoholic beverages. Prohibition, as it was called, was a disaster. Vast fortunes were made through illegal sales of alcohol, and in 1933 Prohibition was repealed.

The Kennedys were Catholics which made their involvement in national politics difficult as there was much anti-Catholic, and anti-Irish, prejudice in a nation still dominated by white Anglo-Saxon Protestants. In 1928 anti-Catholic prejudice told heavily against Al Smith in his unsuccessful bid for the presidency. In 1960 Kennedy was to be only the second Catholic presidential candidate.

John Kennedy grew up in the America of Franklin D. Roosevelt's 'New Deal' when for the first time the power of the state was used to mitigate the effects of the Depression that started in 1929. His father was a personal friend of President Roosevelt who secured Joseph's appointment as Ambassador to Britain. Like many of his fellow countrymen, Joseph P. Kennedy was an isolationist who did not want the United States to become involved in European politics. He supported Britain's **appeasement** of Nazi Germany but in 1940, after the defeat of France, Ambassador Kennedy

> **KEYWORD**
>
> Appeasement: meaning a policy of trying to reach an accommodation with another state. In the 1930s successive British governments were accused by critics of condoning German aggression by carrying appeasement too far. Appeasement became a dirty word in the USA after 1945.

was convinced that Britain was finished. His defeatism made him unpopular in London and he was subsequently replaced. But John, a graduate of Harvard, spent some time as a student at the London School of Economics during which time he produced a critique of appeasement called 'Why Britain Slept'. Unlike his father, the younger Kennedy was an internationalist who came to believe that the United States should play a global role.

Despite his friendship with President Roosevelt, Joseph P. Kennedy was a social conservative, and his racial attitudes reflected the prejudices of his time. By contrast, John Kennedy, a man who had, like all his siblings a $1 million trust fund in his name, grew up with a social conscience. Given his privileged background, Kennedy might have been expected to find a natural home in the **Republican Party**, but his experience as a politician was to give him an appreciation of the inequalities in American society, especially where race was concerned.

FATHER AND SON

There is no doubt that Joseph P. Kennedy had a profound influence on all his children. He was ruthless in pushing their careers and was determined that one of his sons would be president. Until he died in a plane crash in World War Two, the assumption was that the eldest son, Joseph P. Kennedy Junior, would run for president. On his brother's death in 1944, John Kennedy became the focus of the family's political ambitions.

> **KEYWORD**
>
> Republicans and Democrats: by the 1930s the Republicans had emerged as the party of big business and the rich. Roosevelt (President 1933–45) created a Democratic coalition of trade unionists, blacks, Irish and Jewish Americans and the poorer classes.

Kennedy was not as ruthless as his father, who once arranged for a frontal lobotomy to be performed on his mentally retarded daughter without even consulting Rose Kennedy. Nevertheless, it would be wrong to think that John lived in his father's shadow. Both men were highly sexed and reputedly shared lovers, but that was where any resemblance ended. Their temperaments were quite different with the younger Kennedy being both quieter and more cultured than his father. As President, John Kennedy was to remark that he had never seen his father reading a serious book. He certainly never brooked any political interference, even if he was grateful for Ambassador Kennedy's money and political contacts in the **Democratic Party**. And in his own right, John Kennedy was a war hero, injured when his PT boat was cut in two by a Japanese warship leaving the young man with permanent back pain.

THE KENNEDY FAMILY

If Joseph P. Kennedy was the dominant influence in the family (until he suffered a serious stroke in 1961), its other striking feature was a tenacious loyalty and clannishness, often a feature of Irish families. If it was clear that John Kennedy was to be President, the task of his brothers Robert and Edward was to help him achieve that goal. This was equally true of the Kennedy sisters, Eunice, Kathleen (tragically killed in a plane crash in 1948), Jean and Patricia. And it was to be true also of John's wife Jacqueline and Bobby's wife Ethel.

John Kennedy married the cultured and beautiful Jacqueline Bouvier in 1954. Initially she showed little interest in political rough-housing, and limited her involvement to intellectual tasks like translating French books on Indo-China for him. But even Jackie, as she was commonly known, was persuaded to campaign for her husband, and to reluctantly take part in the famous games of touch football at the family holiday home at Hyannis Port.

With this devoted, well-funded, private army behind him, John F. Kennedy became successively a Congressman (1946) and a Senator (1952) before obtaining his party's vice-presidential **nomination** in 1956. Kennedy emerged with credit from the campaign, even though the Democrats lost, and developed the momentum to help him with the presidential nomination in 1960.

THE 1960 CAMPAIGN

By 1959 John Kennedy's intention to run for president was well known. It was also known that the Republican contender was likely to be Vice-President Richard M. Nixon, or 'Tricky Dicky' as he was known to his political opponents.

KEYWORD

Nomination: in the US electoral system, Republican and Democratic contenders have to be nominated by their parties at a convention normally in July or August. Each US state has a number of votes at the convention, and sends a delegation to it. The candidate with the largest vote at the convention becomes the presidential candidate in the November election.

The Kennedy campaign did not lack for cash or charisma. Jacqueline Kennedy, in particular, proved to be an electoral asset even in a poor state like West Virginia, where the Kennedys feared that their wealth and privilege might be provocative. But the Catholic issue dogged John Kennedy throughout the campaign, as opponents attempted to portray him as a stooge of the Pope. Kennedy was adamant in his denial that his religion had any influence on his politics, or most pertinently on any decisions he was likely to make in the White House.

His main opponent for the Democratic nomination was Senator Hubert Humphrey of Minnesota, an experienced politician who lacked the funds available to the Kennedys for the by now all-important TV and radio advertising. By the time the Democratic Convention met on 9 July 1960, it was clear that Kennedy was going to take the nomination. He duly did so on the first ballot, and chose Lyndon Baines Johnson of Texas as his vice-presidential running mate. Johnson, a Southerner who had been Majority Party Leader in the Senate, provided what Kennedy lacked, appeal in the Southern states and a remarkable ability to fix deals in the Congress. Anti-Catholic prejudice was strong in the South, and the Kennedys were also suspected of being sympathetic to the cause of black Civil Rights. The great black American leader, Martin Luther King, who had battled for years against segregation in the South, had endorsed Kennedy's Presidential candidacy. Segregation had blighted US politics since the end of the Civil War in 1865. It:

KEYWORD

Congress: the US Congress or parliament consists of two elected chambers. The lower house is the House of Representatives, and the upper house is the Senate. The US President, unlike the British prime minister, is not a member of the law-making body.

* discriminated against blacks in employment, education and housing

* prevented them exercising their voting rights

* encouraged the existence of racist, fascist-style bodies like the Ku Klux Klan

* stimulated a massive migration of southern blacks to the industrial states of the North

* brought about the setting up of organizations like the National Association for the Advancement of Coloured People (NAACP).

Kennedy in fact had not established himself as an open opponent of segregation, and the previous Eisenhower administration had made some legal moves against the segregationists. But he was certainly able to attract more black votes than Nixon.

THE TV DEBATES

A new feature of the 1960 presidential campaign was the series of **television debates** between the rival candidates. It was Kennedy, the lesser known of the two candidates, who gained most from the national exposure on TV. It was agreed that there would be four debates which would be carried by both television and radio networks. Both men would field questions by selected journalists. The first debate in late September was crucial, and it was generally agreed that Kennedy had won it (although, interestingly, polls showed that radio listeners thought Nixon

> **KEYWORD**
>
> TV debate: the 1960 election was pioneering in allowing the rival candidates to be seen in debate against one another. When Nixon stood again in 1968, he would not agree to further debates. They could still be decisive as, for example, in 1980 when Reagan beat Carter.

had won). Appearances were decisive. Kennedy seemed relaxed and his tan contrasted with Nixon's paleness and 'five o'clock shadow'. Aides hadn't realised that the more swarthy Nixon might be disadvantaged in this way. The Republican contender was also unfortunate in another way. He had injured his knee in an accident earlier in the campaign and had just come out of hospital. He had lost weight and looked pallid and unhealthy. By contrast, Kennedy seemed vigorous and well prepared. In such a closely fought election, this gave him an important advantage against his better-known opponent who had been Vice-President for eight years. Fewer people watched the last three TV debates, but the initial positive impression made by John Kennedy was maintained.

Kennedy needed this advantage in what was to be the closest election in American history. When the election result became known on 8 November 1960, he had beaten Richard Nixon by 303 votes to 219 in the **Electoral College**. But in the head-to-head popular vote, Kennedy won by a wafer-thin margin. Some 48 million Americans voted, but Kennedy beat Nixon by only 120,000 votes. And there were some doubts about those in Chicago where the Democratic Mayor, Richard Daley, was accused of rigging the election in some wards. To his credit though, Nixon put national unity ahead of electoral gain, and did not contest the election. John F. Kennedy had become the first Catholic to be elected President of the United States, but it brought out the Catholic vote in the industrial North. Neither did it prevent many blacks and Jews from voting for him. Kennedy called on his supporters to help him in 'building America, moving America, picking this country of ours up, and sending it into the sixties'.

KEYWORD

Electoral College: in the US electoral systems, there are effectively two elections. One is for the popular vote and the candidate who gets the most votes wins. But the second is the Electoral College, each state having a number of votes according to size. It is possible (as in 2000) for a candidate to win the most votes and lose the election, because a winning candidate *must* win the Electoral College Vote.

2 JFK in the White House

John Kennedy brought a new glamorous ethos to the **White House** from the moment of his **inauguration** in January 1961. In his inaugural speech, he told the audience that political power has been passed to a new generation of Americans who would 'pay any price, bear any burden, meet any hardship, support any friend, oppose any foe to assure the survival and success of liberty'. Kennedy was only 43 when he became President and he represented youth and vitality (the electorate was unaware that he suffered from Addison's disease, which forced him to take large doses of cortisone for adrenal deficiency). He had a beautiful and intelligent wife, and was the first President for many years to bring small children into the White House. He was also the first Catholic President. All these things made JFK distinctively different from his predecessors.

KEYWORDS

White House: The name of the President's mansion comes down to us from the Anglo–American war of 1812. The British burned the original building which was then repainted white to cover the burn damage.

Inauguration: The process by which a new President comes into office, and is sworn in by the US Chief Justice.

He was also something of an outsider. The New York establishment, which had often provided staff for incoming presidents, was somewhat suspicious of the Kennedys. Joseph P. Kennedy was not part of the East coast establishment and his dubious reputation and association with illegal alcohol sales during the Prohibition era influenced the way his son was perceived also. Religion was an additional problem and this could have made the so-called **transition** to power difficult. Kennedy had his own contacts, but they were largely Democratic politicians or academic intellectuals like the historian, Arthur Schlesinger Junior. Through his wife Jackie, he had also come to know people in the theatre, writing and high society. But he did not know many bankers, industrialists, engineers or scientists. Or businessmen who had a very high profile in the previous Eisenhower administration.

This fact could have made the transition very difficult as Kennedy had some 1200 posts to fill, but he made it known that he was prepared to be flexible. In a typically laid-back Kennedy aside, the President told an aide that he didn't care 'whether a man is a Democrat or an Igorot. I want the best fellow I can get for the particular job'. As it was the New York establishment decided to rally around the new administration and he got his men (and on occasion women) appointed.

KEYWORD

Transition: The process by which the new US administration appoints key staff to replace those of the outgoing president between November and January.

THE KEY NEW FRONTIERSMEN

Just as Franklin D. Roosevelt spoke of a 'New Deal', John F. Kennedy referred to a 'New Frontier'. There was supposed to be a new broom in government with new men who had a certain style. There were, as always in American politics, some survivors from previous administrations, but there were also key new staff who were to work closely with the new President. Among his personal White House Staff were Pierre Salinger, the Press Secretary, Ken O'Donnell and Lawrence O'Brien. Arthur Schlesinger and Ted Sorenson (both of whom later wrote celebrated accounts of the Kennedy Presidency) were to be Kennedy's speech writers, while Defence Secretary, Bob McNamara, on leave from the Ford Motor Company, was to become a personal confidante. The noted economist, J.K. Galbraith, was another notable capture for the Kennedy administration as Ambassador to India.

A major issue remained. What was to be done with Bobby Kennedy who had been the President's right-hand man in the victorious election campaign? At first, Kennedy wanted to make Bobby Under-Secretary for Defence under Bob McNamara and was anxious to avoid any accusations of nepotism which would arise if Bobby got one of the top jobs. Joseph P. Kennedy was keen that Bobby should be in a leading position in the administration, but Bobby himself was unenthusiastic about his father's suggestion that he should be **Attorney-General**. He had already had a high profile as Counsel for the Senate 'anti-rackets committee' and wanted a job away from the law. Other candidates for the job, however, turned it down.

A family battle followed with a reluctant brother on one side of the President, and an insistent father on the other. After six weeks of pressure, Bobby Kennedy reluctantly gave way and agreed to take on the crucial job of Attorney-General. In this position he was to be his brother's closest and most trusted adviser. As always with the Kennedys, blood ties counted for everything, but Bobby's presence in the Justice Department was to prove vital in the Kennedy years. Firstly, because his commitment to black civil rights was greater than his brother's, and secondly, because the old dinosaur, J. Edgar Hoover, remained in charge of the **Federal Bureau of Investigation**. President Kennedy would like to have sacked Hoover but dared not because the FBI Chief had files on both his own and his father's sexual escapades. Hoover, who had been running the FBI since the 1920s, was a law unto himself, but no US President dared take him on. Bobby did, however, daring to order the veteran Hoover to attend his office for an interview, something that was virtually unheard of in previous administrations! On another occasion, when meeting with Hoover, the new Attorney-General entertained himself by throwing darts into a dart board not far from Hoover's head. Not surprisingly, Hoover's loathing for the Kennedys was sharpened by this apparent slight to his status.

KEYWORDS

Attorney-General: the leading law officer in the USA. Unlike in the British system, the US Attorney-General has no seat in the Congress.

Federal Bureau of Investigation: the FBI was created to prevent criminals escaping across state lines and so evading justice. Certain crimes (like kidnapping) became federal crimes and were dealt with by FBI agents.

THE FIRST LADY

Another striking characteristic of The Kennedy White House was the high-profile role played by Jacqueline Kennedy. Mrs Kennedy did not enjoy the cut and thrust of politics, and neither did she naturally fit in with the rough-house atmosphere among the Kennedy siblings. But she was a cultured, well dressed and highly attractive woman who contrasted strongly with the rather dowdy image presented by Mrs Eisenhower.

Jackie Kennedy presided over extensive renovation of the White House and was soon conducting TV reporters around it, something that would have been unheard of in the Truman and Eisenhower years.

The idea that the Kennedy White House could be compared to King Arthur's court at Camelot owed a good deal to Jackie Kennedy's glamorous image. This was something that President Kennedy was well aware of, and played up to in his contacts with the general public. Like the President, Jackie came from a Catholic family, in this case the Bouviers who felt excluded from mainstream establishment America. John V. Bouvier III, Jackie's father, was a rich, domineering businessman who ensured that his daughter (born in 1929) received the sort of education well-bred girls required at Vassar. She then took a degree at George Washington University before becoming a photographer for the Washington *Times-Herald* newspaper. Her life changed when she met Jack Kennedy in 1952. 'All I want to do,' she told a woman friend, 'is get married to Jack.'

Kennedy appreciated the fact that Jacqueline had style and intelligence (and French good enough to translate reports on French Indo-China for him when he visited it in the early 1950s). Both proved to be an asset in the White House, and Kennedy appreciated that the crowds that flocked around them on national tours came to see Jackie more than they came to see him.

A DAY IN THE KENNEDY WHITE HOUSE

President Kennedy's day began at 7.30 a.m. when he read the morning papers. The President often made telephone calls as a result of what he read and could make as many as 50 phone calls a day. After a bath and a shave, Kennedy would have breakfast at about 8.45, sometimes with his wife and family (Caroline and John Jr were an important part of his life). On other occasions, the President would breakfast with Congressional leaders or members of his staff. More rarely he would breakfast in bed while reading the papers.

Between 9 and 9.30, Kennedy would arrive at the **Oval Office**, read CIA (**Central Intelligence Agency**) briefings about world trouble spots and then start the daily process of conferences. These would be officially scheduled by his staff, but Kennedy had to be flexible enough to squeeze in a lot of informal conversations with aides. 'The more people I can see,' Kennedy said, 'the more effective I can be as President.'

Every government department was obliged to send John Kennedy a weekly report on their activities. This was a President who wanted to know to an extent that surprised other White House professionals. He also liked to get out and about, whether it be to visit military, space or atomic installations.

KEYWORDS

Oval Office: The office of the President of the United States in the White House.

Central Intelligence Agency: The US governmental agency responsible for espionage abroad. Its headquarters is in Langley, Virginia.

But exercise was also important to the President. Every lunch-time, he went for a swim with his friend and aide Dave Powers. He also had a rigorous exercise programme designed to deal with an ongoing back problem which resulted from the war-time episode when his PT boat was cut in half by a Japanese destroyer. He was obliged to take steroids and this could make him puffy in the face (a contrast with the lean and hungry-looking Bobby). But despite suffering from Addison's disease and a bad back, John Kennedy was generally a (invariably tanned) fit-looking man. He was also a sharp dresser favouring, people noticed, dark-coloured suits with a monogrammed shirt and a PT-boat tie clasp (his Navy service was important to him). Kennedy was aware of the status associated with his office, and would not allow himself to be photographed without a coat and normally a tie.

The President's afternoon meetings tended to be longer and often overran. He was businesslike, preferring to keep comments short, and doodled on a pad while briefings were made by Cabinet colleagues or staff aides.

The long presidential day could drag on until 8.30 p.m. before the President returned for dinner. Even then aides like Ted Sorenson noted that Kennedy was still reading memos and reports until midnight. When films were screened for family and staff, the President would often leave after 15 minutes and return to the Oval Office to work. His Saturdays were also occupied with work, but Sundays were kept free for the family unless a crisis blew up. Sorenson estimated that Kennedy worked an average of 45 to 55 hours a week in the White House. He was not a workaholic leader in the Margaret Thatcher mould, but then he was able to delegate in a way she could not. Fitness would remain a priority, and Kennedy would always try to take a second swim in the evening. And he was careful to take a two-hour long break which allowed him time to exercise while maintaining a much more hands-on style of executive management than the present **incumbent** George W. Bush. Kennedy's predecessor, Dwight Eisenhower, is now accepted by historians as not being the rather indolent President of myth. Nevertheless, the Kennedys were amazed to find indentations in the Oval Office carpet where 'Ike' had been practising his golf swing!

KEYWORD

Incumbent: the word used to describe someone who is currently President of the United States.

THE MEDIA

The Kennedys had always appreciated the value of the media. They had plenty of money to lavish on media campaigns, of course. Referring to his son's 1960 Presidential campaign, Ambassador Kennedy had remarked, 'We'll sell him like soapflakes.' JFK himself was fascinated by the media, especially by Hollywood, and aspired to have the popularity of Hollywood stars.

Nevertheless, the new President managed to maintain a veneer of intellectualism, which contrasted with his predecessor, and was admired by the Washington press corps. He also had a sense of humour which made his press conferences relaxed and friendly occasions. By contrast, Kennedy's successors, Johnson and Nixon, had unhappy relations with the press. Kennedy's press aide, Pierre Salinger, oiled the wheels, but he had a natural easy way with reporters. The President was also a good performer on television, one of the reasons he had won the hard-fought 1960 Presidential campaign.

But Kennedy could become paranoid about the print media. He disliked the way *Time Magazine* wrote about his administration, often complaining directly to its famous owner, Henry Luce. He, as Arthur Schlesinger has noted, cared what was written about him. He expected staff to read papers as carefully as he did, and could be oversensitive about what he read. But he maintained a sense of humour about criticism saying, when asked what he thought about the press in 1962, that he was 'reading it more and enjoying it less'.

THE PRESIDENTIAL IMAGE

John F. Kennedy was a President who knew his history. He was aware of the aura that had surrounded Franklin Roosevelt in the 1930s and 1940s and, according to one source, liked the idea of being seen as a streamlined **FDR**. He wanted to be seen in heroic terms and was concerned about what posterity would think of him. But he was to be a much more cautious president than Roosevelt, who began his Presidency with a legislative onslaught known as 'The Hundred Days' designed to re-activate the US economy.

KEYWORD

FDR (Franklin Delano Roosevelt): Roosevelt was often known by his initials, FDR, just as Kennedy was commonly referred to as JFK.

Nevertheless, Kennedy remained concerned that the image he left to history was a positive one, and it was no accident that he appointed Arthur Schlesinger as one of his aides. Schlesinger had written a three-volume study of the Roosevelt Presidency, and Kennedy knew that he was going to write his account of the Kennedy years as well. He reasoned that if Schlesinger was going to do this, he might as well do it as a 'co-conspirator'. Above all, John Kennedy wanted his legacy to be a positive one, and he would almost certainly have vetted Schlesinger's book had he lived (a biography of him published *before* the 1960 election by James MacGregor Burns was subjected to severe editing by both JFK and Ted Sorenson).

3 Kennedy and the Battle for Civil Rights

The history of the black race in the United States is a long and sad one. A civil war had to be fought in the 1860s to secure the freedom of black slaves (who had been taken from their African homeland), and even then this freedom was theoretical rather than real. Discrimination against black people was widespread in the Southern states, and even when millions of blacks migrated North, they were still the victims of racist attitudes if not legal discrimination as in the South. John Kennedy, as a privileged young white man, had little experience of dealing with blacks before he became President and, it has to be admitted, not much of a record in trying to secure better conditions for them.

THE CIVIL RIGHTS MOVEMENT

There had long been those in the black community, like W.E. du Bois, who had challenged white supremacy in the USA. But the real constitutional challenge to white racism came in the 1950s when some landmark judgements were made. In 1954 in particular the US **Supreme Court** ruled that segregation of children in US schools was illegal in the case Brown versus the Topeka School Board (brought by the NAACP). Even with the Supreme Court on its side the black minority was still confronted by racist officials and politicians in states such as Arkansas, Mississippi, Georgia and Alabama. Notoriously in Alabama there was segregation in public transport but the situation was challenged in 1955 when a black woman, Rosa Parkes, refused to give up her seat in the 'whites only' part of a local bus. This sparked off a black boycott of the bus company in

> ## KEYWORD
>
> The Supreme Court: the highest court in the US is the Supreme Court which can rule on whether or not actions by states or individuals breach the US Constitution.

Montgomery, Alabama which was led by the Reverend Martin Luther King, a Baptist Minister and disciple of **Gandhi**. King was to become the best-known black leader of what became known as the Civil Rights Movement.

KEYWORD

Gandhi: the leader of the Indian independence movement was Mahatma Gandhi who advocated non-violence.

KENNEDY AND THE BLACK COMMUNITY

As a politician, John F. Kennedy had not shown any great interest in the civil rights issue before 1960, and even during the election campaign he had not stressed the issue. Some efforts were made to win the black vote, however, and when Martin Luther King was imprisoned in Atlanta, Georgia after a civil rights march, Kennedy phoned his wife to offer support. Bobby Kennedy followed this up by phoning the judge involved in the case, and this joint action by the brothers helped secure Doctor King's early release. As a result, Luther King's father switched his vote from Nixon to Kennedy and many other black voters followed suit. But many white voters remained unaware of what the Kennedy brothers had done. Campaign aides feared that such a move might actually have cost white votes. But Kennedy himself, now convinced of Martin Luther King's importance as a national figure, decided to make the call. 'What the hell,' he is reported to have said. 'That's the decent thing to do. Why not? Get her on the phone.' It needs to be stressed, however, that Kennedy's civil rights record at this point was no better than Nixon's, although King and his aides regarded him as sympathetic.

But Kennedy was increasingly aware of the fact that blacks had only second-class status in the US. During the 1960 campaign he had made a speech in which he warned that, 'The Negro baby has one-half regardless of his talents, statistically one-half as much chance of finishing high school as the white baby.'

He also came to realize that if he was elected President, he could end discrimination in federal housing programmes with the stroke of a pen by **executive action**. This had been something that Eisenhower had been unwilling to do, probably fearing that he would lose support in the segregationist South which had voted for him in the 1952 and 1956 presidential elections. It was certainly true that in the 1960 election, if whites alone had voted, Nixon would have won a decisive 52 per cent of the vote. Kennedy's problem was that as President, he lacked the votes in the Congress to enact really decisive civil rights legislation, and could only act alone on limited issues like housing.

KENNEDY'S CIVIL RIGHTS POLICY

When Kennedy entered the White House in 1961, he had a three-pronged civil rights strategy:

* there would be a clear presidential commitment to civil rights

* blacks would be appointed to government posts

* both the White House and the Justice Department would take vigorous action on the civil rights issue.

To underline the commitment, the new Attorney-General, Robert Kennedy, along with other administration members, resigned from the Metropolitan Club in Washington because of its discrimination against blacks. The President himself made an executive order against discrimination in federal employment, and blacks were appointed as Assistant Secretary of Labour and Commissioner for the **District of Columbia**. He had, nevertheless, to do a delicate balancing act. Civil rights reform was unpopular in the South, and Kennedy needed Southern support to get other parts of his programme through the Congress. Kennedy was well aware of the injustice meted out to blacks, but as a politician to his fingertips, he also had to concentrate on what was practical. This needs to be remembered when we try to assess what appears to be a disappointing Kennedy record in the field of civil rights. There is no doubt though that President Kennedy, like his Vice-President Lyndon Johnson, was committed to improving the lot of black men and women. Johnson was put in charge of a special presidential equal opportunities committee. It was also true that with crises like the Bay of Pigs on his hands in the early days, John Kennedy left much of the action on civil rights to Bobby.

He, in his usual zealous way, immediately began a campaign to recruit more blacks into the Justice Department. For the first time also they were appointed as United States attorneys. Where segregation in the South was concerned, Kennedy and his colleagues were prepared to use the law courts to force the admission of black students into all-white schools and colleges.

Even more important was the issue of voting rights in the South where, ever since the Civil War ended in 1865, blacks were prevented from exercising their right to vote. Sometimes this was a result of outright intimidation applied by the Ku Klux Klan (an overtly racist organization which also hated communists and Catholics). In other instances impossible literacy tests, which most whites would have failed, were used to stop blacks from voting. Robert Kennedy and the Justice Department brought legal suits against Southern authorities that refused to register blacks for the vote. At the same time, black civil rights leaders were encouraged to get their people, the victims of decades of racist thuggery and violence, to turn out in elections.

Increasingly, however, black civil rights activists and their liberal white supporters took action on their own, sending so-called '**freedom riders**' into the segregationist South. This reflected some impatience with the pace of change initiated by the Kennedy brothers. Nevertheless, such groups still needed federal protection. When freedom riders arrived in Montgomery,

KEYWORD

Freedom riders: young activists who challenged segregation in restaurants, waiting rooms and bus depots.

Alabama in May 1961, they were set upon by a thousand-strong white mob. John Seigenthaler, Robert Kennedy's special assistant, sent by him to report on the situation, was attacked and knocked unconscious. The Attorney-General was forced to send 600 federal marshals to Montgomery to put an end to such intimidation.

THE MEREDITH CASE

The most celebrated civil rights case of the Kennedy years was the one concerning James Meredith in the state of Mississippi, arguably the most racist state in the Union. John Kennedy himself was to be directly involved in its resolution. The sequence of events was as follows:

* James Meredith, an Air Force veteran, applied for admission to the University of Mississippi

* the university used complex academic arguments to reject his application

* a federal court ruled that Meredith had been rejected 'solely because he was a Negro'

* on appeal, that court's decision was upheld.

Meredith was determined to go ahead with his application, but the loud-mouthed segregationist, Ross Barnett, Governor of Mississippi, personally prevented Meredith from registering in June 1962. White racists marched about the university campus singing 'Glory, glory, segregation'. Barnett used the old-fashioned doctrine of **nullification** to justify his actions.

> **KEYWORD**
>
> Nullification: the supposed right of state officials to prevent any outside body, e.g. the federal government, from usurping power in the State.

President Kennedy was disturbed by the television pictures he saw coming from Mississippi. Southern racism was now making an exhibition of itself for all the world to see, and he felt bound to intervene. Kennedy had several conversations with Barnett focusing on his ability to keep order on the campus in Oxford, Mississippi, and Meredith's legal right to be registered at the university. Kennedy went on national television, assuming that Barnett would obey federal instructions and back down. He told the TV audience that if the federal government could be defied in this way, 'then no law would stand free from doubt, no judge would be sure of his writ, and no citizen would be safe from his neighbours'.

But unknown to Kennedy, the situation in Oxford had worsened and federal marshals were under attack from an enraged mob of students and local residents shouting '2-4-1-3. We hate Ken-ne-dy'. At this point, US army troops had to be sent in. Meredith was registered the next day but two lives had been lost in the fighting. Even then the courageous Meredith spent months being escorted by federal marshals to his classes, and ostracized by white students. From President Kennedy's point of view, the James Meredith case was crucial because:

* it established the principle that the federal government would not tolerate such discrimination

* it resolved black doubts about the level of his commitment to civil rights (a Harris poll shortly afterwards put Kennedy behind only the NAACP and Martin Luther King as having done most for civil rights).

Black leaders did not know how edgy Kennedy, the politician, still was about the civil rights issue. He was on friendly terms, for example, with the black entertainer Sammy Davis Jr (part of the famous Hollywood 'ratpack' of the 1960s which included Frank Sinatra and his brother-in-law Peter Lawford) but was appalled at the prospect of him turning up at the White House with his white wife, the Swedish actress Mai Britt. Kennedy was afraid that photos of the mixed race couple might cost him votes.

Nonetheless, three points had emerged about the civil rights issue by the autumn of 1962:

* the federal courts were ready to define black rights

* the blacks themselves were determined to claim them

* some white Southerners, including local police forces, were prepared to go to extreme lengths to stop them doing so.

This became alarmingly clear in April 1963 when another confrontation involving Martin Luther King took place in Birmingham, Alabama, notorious as the race hate capital of the South. King was launching a big campaign against discrimination in shops, restaurants and jobs but the protesters ran into the obdurate person of local Police Chief, Eugene 'Bull' Connor. Police dogs and fire hoses were used on the protesters and, yet again, King was arrested. In the end, some 500 black protesters, many just young high-school students, ended up in Birmingham's jails.

Kennedy professed himself sickened by the pictures from Alabama, but he had no powers to intervene as no federal law had been infringed. He asked for patience, although conceding that he could 'well understand why the Negroes of Birmingham are tired of being asked to be patient'. The situation grew tenser as black houses were firebombed. The breakdown in law and order then allowed President Kennedy to send in federal troops. Connor and his uniformed bigots were forced to back down.

There were fears of a **white backlash** but the momentum of events was with the Civil Rights Movement. There were still battles to fight, though. In May, a federal judge ruled that the University of Alabama must admit two black students. Governor George Wallace, following Barnett's example in Mississippi, vowed to stop

KEYWORD

White backlash: a term used in the 1960s to suggest that whites might react against civil rights reform.

this. Again, there were to be TV pictures of a state governor trying to obstruct the entry of black students onto university premises. John Kennedy reacted to this provocation by federalizing part of the

Alabama **National Guard**. But by the time the National Guard arrived at the campus at Tuscaloosa, Wallace had decided to obey Kennedy's instruction not to obstruct integration. That evening on national television, Kennedy told his audience that the USA had been founded on the principle of

> **KEYWORD**
>
> **National Guard:** a part-time militia in the American states used to deal with civil emergencies.

equality and 'that the rights of every man are diminished when the rights of one man are threatened'. There could be no pretence of equality in America when blacks were being treated as second-class citizens.

Just how far America had to travel in the field of race relations was demonstrated that very same night when Medgar Evers, friend and adviser to James Meredith, was shot dead by a white racist in Jackson, Mississippi. John Kennedy responded by inviting Evers's wife, children and brother-in-law to the White House a week later. Bobby Kennedy told Charles Evers, the brother-in-law of the dead man, to ring him any time day or night on civil rights-related issues (Charles had taken Medgar's place as head of the Mississippi NAACP). More and more meetings were scheduled with black leaders by the Kennedy brothers although some (like the meeting between Bobby and the bitterly critical writer James Baldwin) were tense. Both men were shocked by the degree of bitterness shown by some black leaders who were suspicious of all whites, and impatient with the pace of change.

John F. Kennedy's friend and biographer, Arthur Schlesinger Jr, was to write that 'May and June 1963 were exciting months for a historian'. It is easy to see why he wrote this because those two months brought the question of black rights before the nation as never before. Demonstrations and sit-ins were commonplace and on 19 June, Kennedy sent his long-awaited Civil Rights Bill to the Congress for approval. It was rather limited in scope, merely making federal funds available to help the voluntary desegregation of schools. Kennedy was worried about his Southern white constituency but the battle there was already lost, so great was the hatred against the President because of his perceived encouragement of black civil rights.

THE WASHINGTON MARCH

The big event as far as the Civil Rights Movement was concerned in the summer of 1963 was the huge demonstration organized for August in Washington. It had two main aims:

* to put pressure on the administration to make further reforms

* to put pressure on the Congress where a **filibuster** was expected from Southern opponents of civil rights.

KEYWORD

Filibuster: a tactic used in the Congress whereby a series of speakers deliberately waste time to stop legislation being passed.

Kennedy was not enthused by the prospect of hundreds of thousands of civil rights demonstrators descending on Washington, and tried to persuade Martin Luther King to call off the demonstration. He refused to do so. Bobby Kennedy also tried to persuade King to abandon the March on Washington, arguing that there would be clashes with American Nazis and members of the Ku Klux Klan.

Both Kennedy brothers watched on television as King made his famous 'I have a dream' speech to a quarter of a million people in front of the Lincoln Memorial. He told his enthusiastic audience of his hope that 'on the red hills of Georgia the sons of former slaves and the sons of former slave-owners will be able to sit together at the table of brotherhood …'. The vast crowd went on to sing the old Baptist hymn which had become synonymous with the Civil Rights Movement:

> We shall overcome, we shall overcome
> We shall overcome, some day
> Oh deep in my heart, I do believe
> We shall overcome some day.

The Kennedys, hard-bitten politicians both, were duly impressed. There was no serious law and order problem.

KING AND THE FBI

Martin Luther King worried President Kennedy in other ways which had nothing to do with the sheer size of his public support. One concerned the attitude of that old enemy of the Kennedys, FBI Chief J. Edgar Hoover. Hoover was a racist who loathed King and all he stood for, but he also had damaging information about the President's sexual promiscuity. So when Hoover claimed that Levinson, Luther King's closest white friend, was a Soviet agent, Kennedy was obliged to listen. The FBI had already placed **bugs** in Levinson's office. Kennedy spoke to King about the Levinson problem two months before the Washington March, and also warned him that he himself was under observation by the FBI. In fact, as both the Kennedys knew, there was no serious evidence that Levinson was a spy, but the slightest rumour that King had a communist aide could do them serious damage in the South where simplistic links were often made between communism and black civil rights. Under pressure from Hoover, the Kennedys took action against King. His lawyer's phone had a wire tap placed on it, and Bobby Kennedy considered authorizing a tap on King's phone also, before changing his mind.

> ## KEYWORDS
>
> **Bug:** The colloquial expression for wire taps. The placing of such taps on someone's telephone.
>
> **Mafia:** The shadowy criminal organization that originated in Sicily and was exported to the USA.

As ever with the Kennedys, sexual indulgence contributed to their problems. Hoover had told the President that he knew about his sexual liaison with Judith Campbell who was also the mistress of the **Mafia** boss, Sam Giancana. They apparently did not know that Hoover was a long-time closet homosexual who dressed up in women's clothes in private, information that would have ruined Hoover had it become public. As it was, three months later Hoover pressurized Robert Kennedy into authorizing taps on Martin Luther King as well. They revealed that King too was having extra-marital affairs, thus giving Hoover more grubby material with which to blackmail the Kennedys. They, it must be said, lacked the courage to remove Hoover as FBI chief.

CIVIL RIGHTS: THE KENNEDY LEGACY

In many ways, John Kennedy's legacy was disappointing for black Americans. His commitment was generally not in doubt (although critics like James Baldwin were dismissive) but black leaders felt that civil rights was not given the priority it deserved. Kennedy had a difficult situation in the Congress where Southern Democrats could wreck his programmes by filibustering or withholding their votes, but it has to be admitted that his successor, Lyndon Johnson, had a more dynamic civil rights record. Kennedy, as his aide Theodore Sorenson has conceded, did not understand the depth of black bitterness about discrimination and was sometimes over-cautious in the use of federal power against the segregationists. Defenders of Kennedy would argue that radical civil rights legislation in the early 1960s would have created a Republican-**Dixiecrat** alliance against him in the Congress. But it remains true that it was Robert Kennedy, rather than his brother, who was more sensitive to the demands and sensitivities of the Civil Rights Movement. It was he who said to those who complained about black radicalism that any such person should first say that he 'would willingly change the color of his skin and go and live in a Negro section of a large city'.

KEYWORD

Dixiecrat: the name used for Southern conservative Democrats in Congress. 'Dixie' is a name for the old South.

In summary, therefore, it can be said that:

* there was no doubt that Kennedy was sympathetic to the black cause

* he felt himself hedged in by the threat from the Dixiecrats in the Congress

* radical blacks felt frustrated by the pace of change under Kennedy

* Kennedy had some difficulty in understanding the level of bitterness about discrimination in the black community.

Cuba and the Battle with Fidel Castro

4

THE HISTORICAL BACKGROUND

The association between the United States and the island of Cuba (some 145 kilometres off the coast of Florida) went back to 1898. In that year, the Americans won the Spanish American War and for a further four years, they occupied the island. Even when the Americans left Cuba, they reserved for themselves the right of intervention if, in their judgement, Cuban independence was in danger. The so-called **Monroe Doctrine** also supported the US position, and it also obtained the naval base of Guantanamo on the island.

KEYWORDS

Monroe Doctrine: in 1823, President James Monroe declared that any intervention by non-American states in either North or South America would be deemed a hostile act by Wasington, which could result in war.

Over the years, the USA built up a dominant economic position on the island. By the late 1950s, the Americans owned 40 per cent of the Cuban sugar industry, 80 per cent of its utilities and 90 per cent of the mining industry. The Cuban capital Havana with its night-clubs and gambling casinos had become a playground for rich American tourists and, it was reported, members of the criminal Mafia.

Since 1940, Cuban politics had been dominated by the corrupt dictator Batista who had American backing (a tendency to back corrupt Latin American dictators was a feature of twentieth-century US foreign policy). His secret police terrorized opponents while Batista and his family creamed off much of the island's wealth. But declining demand for Cuban sugar, the island's main export, made the situation worse by throwing thousands out of work. This created opportunities for opponents of the regime.

CASTRO

By the late 1950s the most well-known opponent of Batista was Fidel Castro, the son of a rich landowner from Orente province. Although expensively educated at a private school and a graduate of Havana University, young Fidel turned against his father and the system he represented. As early as 1947 he and other Cubans took part in an unsuccessful attempt to overthrow the dictator Trujillo in the nearby Dominican Republic. Shortly afterwards Castro went to New York and bought copies of Marxist texts such as *Das Kapital*. But he was not yet a convinced communist rather did he, like other Cuban nationalists, want to throw out the corrupt Batista. An attempt to do this in 1953 failed and Castro and his comrades had to flee to Mexico after he had spent 19 months in jail. From there he returned with a handful of followers and set up the **Movement of The Twenty Sixth of July** based in the Sierra Maestra mountains. By 1958 Castro was attracting considerable support even from landowners and businessmen disillusioned by the rampant corruption in Cuba.

US warnings to Batista about his repressive methods were ignored and on New Year's Day 1959 the revolutionaries under Castro forced the dictator and his family to flee. Initially Castro seemed anxious for US support. When he visited the USA in April 1959, he assured the US Senate's **Foreign Relations Committee** that he would not seize US property and that he could handle communist allies in the new Cuban government (both his brother Raul and the soon to be famous Che Guevara were communists). It was also true that, despite American paranoia about the Russians, the USSR knew virtually nothing about the Cuban Revolution.

KEYWORDS

The Movement of the Twenty Sixth of July: Castro's rebel movement took its name from the unsuccessful attack by them on the Moncada barracks at Santiago in July 1953.

The Foreign Relations Committee: the Foreign Relations Committee of the US Senate (the upper house of the US Congress) has an important monitoring role where US foreign policy is concerned.

From that point, however, US–Cuban relations worsened sharply. Castro was anxious to avoid excessive dependence on the US and took a number of measures that produced a somewhat hysterical US response. Neither did Washington seem to understand that the Soviet leader, Nikita Khrushchev, preferred better relations with the United States to flirting with the virtually unknown Castro. A series of tit-for-tat measures therefore followed:

* Castro signed a trade deal with the USSR

* US oil companies refused to process Cuban supplies of Soviet crude petroleum

* Castro seized their refineries in Cuba

* Eisenhower placed a ban on all Cuban sugar exports to the USA

* Castro nationalized all American sugar mills, ranches and refineries on the island of Cuba.

The result of this breakdown in relations was that (predictably) Castro turned to the USSR for economic and military help. Despite his initial reluctance to help Castro, Khrushchev could see that the USSR had a great opportunity to establish communist influence in Cuba and perhaps Latin America as a whole. He therefore agreed to take the whole annual Cuban sugar crop of 711,000 tonnes. In these events lay the genesis of the two acute crises in Cuban–American relations that were to dominate the first two years of the Kennedy Presidency.

JFK AND CUBA

John Kennedy's links with Cuba were superficial. He had visited the island with friends in 1957, during a difficult phase of his marriage, and apparently admired the friendly and vivacious character of the people. But in the 1960 Presidential campaign he had been openly critical of Batista, calling his regime 'one of the most bloody and repressive dictatorships in the long history of Latin American repression'. He was also curious to learn more about the extrovert Castro and what motivated him, asking the US Ambassador in Havana for briefings. It is clear that for much of the period before he actually became President, Kennedy was quite sympathetic towards Castro, asking friends why the US had so consistently backed the corrupt Batista.

But by the autumn of 1960 Kennedy seems to have become a **Cold War Warrior** where Cuba was concerned. He made bellicose statements saying, for example, that 'Castro and his gang have betrayed the ideals of the Cuban revolution'. Castro was also accused of making the island a base for communist infiltration in Latin America. It does seem, however, that at least part of the reason for Kennedy's change of position on Cuba was due to electoral

KEYWORDS

Cold War Warrior: the phrase used to note those who were strongly hostile to the USSR and communism.

Emigré: from the French, meaning an exile from one's country.

considerations. He may well have feared that President Eisenhower and his Vice-President Richard Nixon were planning to oust Castro *before* the November election. This would allow Nixon, a notorious Cold War Warrior himself, to pose as a tough anti-communist leader and gain votes. It is clear from Nixon's 1978 memoirs that the Vice-President was himself convinced that Castro was a communist who had to be overthrown. Nixon also kept demanding to know why the CIA didn't have a plan to get rid of Castro.

THE PLOT AGAINST CASTRO

As early as March 1959, the CIA was examining ways of getting rid of Castro, even before he had opened diplomatic relations with the Soviet Union or seized any American property. This was done with the full knowledge of President Eisenhower, and the favoured option was to use anti-Castro Cuban **emigrés** based in Miami against him. The same technique had been used successfully against the allegedly communist (but in fact democratic) government of Arbenz in Guatemala when it threatened to take over US property in 1954. This plan was being refined by the CIA throughout 1960, although Eisenhower dragged his feet about landing an anti-Castro force in Cuba (much to Nixon's irritation). Nevertheless the day before Kennedy's inauguration, Eisenhower felt able to tell his successor that the Cuban project was 'going well'. It was this plan to land a Cuban emigré force on the island that Kennedy inherited when he became President.

Like all successful Presidential candidates, Kennedy had of course been briefed by the CIA, and seemed to approve of the project to remove Castro. By now his dislike of Castro had become so intense that it shocked others, such as the incoming Secretary of State for Foreign Affairs, Dean Rusk. But Kennedy had to wait through Dwight Eisenhower's **lame duck** presidency before he could rid himself of the unwelcome neighbour in the South.

KEYWORD

Lame duck: an American phrase to describe the period between November and January, when the old president is serving out his time before the new president takes over.

Kennedy was, though, cautious about mounting the invasion for a number of reasons, despite his growing personal dislike for the Cuban leader.

* He did not want to seem like an aggressive imperialist attacking a small independent country.

* He did not want to repeat the Soviet experience in Hungary in 1956 where a revolution was bloodily put down.

* There was a danger that Khrushchev might put pressure on the Western weak point in Berlin.

* He realized that the possible involvement of the USSR might trigger off a nuclear war between the two super-powers.

After consultations with his advisers, Kennedy became convinced that the Russians would not in fact react if he mounted an invasion of Cuba. But he insisted that US involvement be minimal. Just six US

B-26 aircraft, with Cuban markings, were given to the anti-Castro rebels which was considerably less than the CIA had originally wanted. There could be no question of US ground forces being involved, as this would trigger off latent Latin American hostility to 'Yankee' imperialism (the US had a long history of military intervention in both Central and South America). All this, however, rested on an assumption that Castro's forces could easily be defeated, and that there would be a popular uprising against him. This assumption proved to be hopelessly misguided. It was a consequence of faulty CIA intelligence, and both Eisenhower and Kennedy were taken in.

THE BAY OF PIGS

In one sense JFK was in a weak position with regard to the intelligence agencies. His problem with FBI Director J. Edgar Hoover has already been referred to, but Kennedy would have been aware that CIA Chief Allen Dulles would also have access to the FBI files about the sexual infidelities of both himself and Ambassador Kennedy. He probably wished to fire Dulles, just as he would have wanted to be rid of Hoover, but could not risk it (and his father insisted that Dulles stay). Kennedy was therefore under additional pressure to accept the Dulles plan to land the anti-Castro force at the **Bay of Pigs**. Yet he was curiously hesitant about giving the green light to the operation. Unusually, he did not inform his brother about the operation until a week before it was launched in April 1961.

KEYWORD

Bay of Pigs or the Cochinas Bay: the site chosen for Kennedy's ill-fated invasion of Cuba in 1961.

From the outset it was clear that the operation was going badly wrong. Within hours, the President was telling Bobby on the telephone, 'I don't think it is going as well as it should'. This proved to be an understatement as it became obvious that the Bay of Pigs landing was an unmitigated disaster. Castro's forces did not prove to be the pushover the CIA predicted, and the invasion force was rapidly destroyed. The President was devastated, but took personal responsibility for the fiasco. The consequences of the failure of the Bay of Pigs operation were that:

* far from being undermined, Castro's authority in Cuba was greatly strengthened

* Khrushchev began to see JFK as a young, inexperienced President who would be susceptible to pressure

* the USSR saw Cuba as a useful base in the Caribbean

* there was a renewed determination in the White House to settle scores with Castro in the near future.

This desire for revenge was immediately evident in the White House as President Kennedy set up a special committee to deal with Castro. He recognized that he had made a mistake in not using Bobby in the planning of the Bay of Pigs operation, and his brother played a dominant role on the new committee. Even more than the President, Bobby was determined to 'get Castro'. Amidst this macho need for revenge, the issue of whether Castro really posed a serious threat to the USA was rather lost sight of. But a number of plans, codenamed **Operation Mongoose**, were hatched by the White House and the CIA to eliminate him. Some were frankly bizarre. They included the idea of sending the Cuban leader a poisoned diving suit (he was known to enjoy scuba diving) and a sea-shell that would explode

KEYWORD

Operation Mongoose: the codename for the US plan to destroy Castro and his regime.

when Castro picked it up. Even odder was the attempt to poison Castro so that his beard would fall out and he would appear to be less virile! It is difficult not to reach the conclusion that the Kennedy brothers showed a lack of judgement and proportion where Castro was concerned. So great was the pressure placed on the CIA to deal with him that one official remarked that 'It's no wonder they came up with some screwball ideas'. As it turned out, all the desperate attempts to get rid of Castro failed completely, and the Kennedy brothers had to wait a long time to even scores with the Cuban dictator.

5 The Cuban Missile Crisis

The origins of the second, greater Cuban crisis of October 1962 lay in the perceptions created by the Bay of Pigs fiasco 18 months before. In the summer of 1961, Kennedy met his Soviet counterpart Nikita Khrushchev at a **Summit** in Vienna, but the meeting was not a success. Khrushchev was an ebullient extrovert who was a complete contrast to his sinister, paranoid predecessor Joseph Stalin. He had visited the USA in 1959 and watched the Can-Can in Hollywood (it was barely imaginable that Stalin would ever have done this), while also absurdly telling Vice-President Nixon in Moscow that the Soviet Union would overtake the USA's living standards and 'wave it bye-bye'. Another example of Khrushchev's extrovert style was when he banged his shoe on the table at the United Nations General Assembly in New York to interrupt Prime Minister Harold MacMillan. Strong-minded, and convinced of the superiority of the Soviet system, Khrushchev believed that he could bully the young American President at the Vienna Summit.

KEYWORDS

Summit: So-called 'summit diplomacy' involving meetings between US and Soviet leaders was a feature of the 1950s and 1960s.

Domino theory: The American belief that the states of South-East Asia were like a row of dominoes. If one went communist, they all would.

There were several prongs to Khrushchev's assault on Kennedy. Firstly, he wanted a test ban treaty but would not agree to the 20 annual inspections of nuclear facilities the Americans wanted. Secondly, he wanted the US and the West out of Berlin where the Potsdam Agreement had allowed them to station troops since 1945. This in turn made West Berlin a democratic enclave right in the heart of communist East Germany. Lastly, Khrushchev objected to US military involvement in the tiny South-East Asian kingdom of Laos, which was a consequence of US belief in the so-called **domino theory**.

No agreement could be reached and the Summit broke up in confusion. Dealing with Khrushchev, Kennedy remarked to an aide, was like 'dealing with Dad – all give and no take'. The President's immediate response after the Summit was to ask the Congress for a $3 billion increase in defence spending, and a crash programme for civil defence to protect US citizens from nuclear attack.

THE BERLIN CRISIS

In Vienna, Kennedy had told a journalist that 'I won't give in to the Russians no matter what happens', and this new resolution was soon to be put to the test. For in August 1961, the East German authorities began to build a wall between their half of Berlin and the democratic Western half of it. In reality, it was a panic measure as thousands of East Germans had been using the absence of physical barriers in the city to flee to the West. This rush westwards had become deeply embarrassing for both the East Germans and the Soviet Union. Kennedy's response, to what seemed for a while to be a threat to West Berlin itself, was to send a convoy of armoured trucks into the city to ensure the right of access. At one point, American and Soviet tanks faced one another across **Checkpoint Charlie**. But ultimately, the crisis fizzled out as there was effectively nothing the West could do about the Wall.

KEYWORD

Checkpoint Charlie: the most famous crossing point between East and West Berlin before the Wall came down in 1990.

Kennedy had shown some resolve, but Khrushchev doesn't seem to have been impressed for he responded in dramatic fashion to Fidel Castro's requests for military assistance. Castro himself was convinced that the Americans were plotting to attack Cuba again. Operation Mongoose seemed to him not a desperate US attempt to destabilize his government but the prelude to a new invasion. Khrushchev agreed with this assessment and this was why he agreed to supply Castro with mid-range ballistic missiles. According to one source, Khrushchev thought that the operation to supply the missiles could be hidden from US intelligence for about two months. It was then calculated that

Kennedy would not wish to tell the American people about them before the Congressional elections in November. After that, Kennedy would be prepared to tolerate the existence of the missiles in Cuba, just as the USSR had to accept the US missile sites in Greece and Turkey. Khrushchev had often complained to the Americans about the existence of such bases so close to Russia's borders. But he had made a woeful miscalculation, although one which JFK may have inadvertently encouraged. When the USSR began nuclear testing again in September (despite a promise given at Vienna that they would not do so), Khrushchev may have seen Kennedy's failure to complain as a sign of weakness. Neither did the President order a resumption of US nuclear testing. But Kennedy may have felt relaxed because he knew by mid-September that the Russians had only about 25 missiles capable of reaching the USA.

By the following March, however, his attitude had changed and Kennedy told the Russians that unless they agreed to a test ban treaty, America would resume nuclear testing. The Soviet response to this was to call off a projected Kennedy–Khrushchev TV debate (it never was to take place).

THE MISSILE CRISIS

Cuba remained at the top of Kennedy's agenda. Indeed, it has been suggested that through Operation Mongoose he sanctioned more **covert** CIA activity than any other American president. Much of this was plainly misguided but his Soviet opponent had been guilty of an even worse miscalculation.

KEYWORDS

Covert: meaning secret. Carried out without public or Congressional knowledge.

U-2: the US intelligence spy plane.

By late July 1962, Khrushchev had authorized the sending of the Soviet missiles to Cuba. Some 5,000 Soviet technicians and specialists were also sent to the island to service the missiles. On 29 August, President Kennedy was told that a **U-2** spy plane had provided clear evidence that **SAM** sites were being constructed. The President now decided to warn off the Russians, telling Khrushchev that if at any stage Cuba became 'an offensive military base of significant capacity for the Soviet Union', the USA would act according to its own security interests. Kennedy and most of his advisers still thought at this stage that Khrushchev would not be reckless enough to place nuclear missiles on Cuba. SAMs, after all, were only for defensive purposes.

> **KEYWORDS**
>
> **SAMs:** Surface-to-air anti-aircraft missiles. Used to defend missile sites.
>
> **Secretary of State:** Shorthand for the Secretary of State for Foreign Affairs. Usually seen as a key post in the US administration.

THE DISCOVERY

Nevertheless, U-2 spy flights over Cuba were increased, but these flights in September produced nothing to prove that Russian intentions were anything more than defensive. There were stories about nuclear installations coming from anti-Castro Cuban refugees in the United States, but these were thought to be unreliable. Right into the first week in October, intelligence reports had produced nothing conclusive to show that nuclear missiles had been placed on Cuba.

All this changed on 14 October 1962, when another U-2 flew a mission (bad weather had delayed it for several days). Blown-up photographs from its flight made it clear that there were missile-launching pads on Cuba. A missile was actually identified on such a pad near San Christóbal.

Kennedy felt deceived. During the weeks since late August when he and Khrushchev had been corresponding privately about nuclear disarmament, the Russians had secretly been supplying Castro with lethal weapons. 14 October was a Sunday. Kennedy convened a Cabinet meeting on the following Tuesday to discuss what had now become a full-blown crisis. The **Secretary of State**, Dean Rusk, observed that the situation 'could well lead to a general war'. Kennedy and his colleagues were confused about Soviet motives. Perhaps Khrushchev was trying to swap Cuba for Berlin? Or perhaps the Russians were not happy with their existing missile system and wanted a base much closer to the US? They might also be making a point about the closeness of American missile bases in Turkey.

Kennedy let his colleagues do most of the talking. His brother Bobby, now at the heart of presidential decision-making, warned that an air strike against Cuba would mean that 'you're going to kill an awful lot of people and we're going to take an awful lot of heat on it'. But at this stage, Kennedy favoured drastic action. He told the Cabinet that 'we're going to take out these missiles'. This reaction showed how shocked he was by Soviet actions. But he accepted, too readily perhaps, the view that Khrushchev would stand by his promise not to send nuclear missiles outside the USSR. After all, the Soviet leader had said during the Bay of Pigs crisis that missiles might be sent to protect Castro. But further confusion was generated by Khrushchev's promise that he would do nothing to embarrass Kennedy during the Congressional elections that were due in the autumn of 1962. All in all though, Kennedy's policy had been heavily influenced by the perception that Khrushchev and the Soviet leadership were inherently cautious.

He was not, though, unduly impressed by arguments in the Cabinet and elsewhere about the Soviet Union violating the Monroe Doctrine. It could easily be argued that the presence of American Jupiter missiles in Turkey was just as provocative as the Soviet missiles being based in Cuba. Indeed, had the USSR made a public statement about sending missiles to defend Cuba, Kennedy might have been caused some embarrassment. As it was, Khrushchev's secrecy was to play into the President's hands, although he also insisted that as few people as possible in the administration knew what the Russians had done. Kennedy therefore set up a so-called Executive Committee (Ex-Comm) to deal with the crisis, whose members would be key Cabinet appointees.

Various options were available to President Kennedy:

* an outright invasion of Cuba and the overthrow of Castro

* a so-called 'surgical' strike aimed only at the nuclear missile bases

* diplomatic pressure on Khrushchev combined with a naval blockade.

But all of them presented real problems. Even a limited air strike, for example, would kill the Russians manning the missiles and could result in a Soviet nuclear response. It might also kill many innocent Cubans and damage the United States' always delicate relationship with Latin America. Equally dangerous was the possibility that American action against Cuba might provoke a Soviet move against the ever vulnerable West Berlin. Military hawks in the Pentagon wanted to use the crisis to get rid of Castro once and for all, but Secretary for Defence, Bob McNamara, put forward the wiser, less hysterical option of a naval blockade. Predictably the military rejected the softer option.

On Thursday 16 October, Kennedy saw the Soviet Foreign Minister Gromyko in the White House. Both men were engaged in a game of bluff. Gromyko knew there were missiles in Cuba but he did not know that Kennedy knew this too. For his part, Kennedy did not want Gromyko to become aware of his knowledge. He merely warned Gromyko that the USA would not tolerate the placing of missiles in Cuba. By now, he was becoming attracted to the idea of a blockade, because it gave Khrushchev the maximum amount of time to back down. On the Friday morning, Bobby Kennedy also came out firmly against the idea of an air strike. His brother was attempting to preserve the impression of normality by doing some political campaigning. He didn't want to see the votes of Ex-Comm for the various options because, he said, 'I may choose the wrong policy, and then the people who are right will have it in writing'.

Kennedy consulted Ex-Comm and he also brought in the **National Security Council** (NSC) for consultations. A week after the discovery of the missile sites though, he still had not come down firmly in favour of any of the options. But he took the possibility of an all-out nuclear war very seriously, asking Jackie whether she would be prepared to join him if he went to Mount Weather, an enormous secret presidential shelter hewn out of a mountain in Virginia. She said that she would prefer to remain with him in the White House shelter should the worst come to the worst. By now, too, Kennedy was informing foreign allies such as France's de Gaulle and Britain's Prime Minister Macmillan about the Soviet missile threat.

KEYWORDS

National Security Council: the specialist defence policy body which advises the President.

Security Council: the UN body which represents the great powers, allowing them to take emergency action when appropriate.

Kennedy and his immediate colleagues were now under immense strain, a point noted by Robert Kennedy in his famous account of the crisis, *Thirteen Days*. 'Each one of us,' he wrote later, 'was being asked to make a recommendation which, if wrong and if accepted, could mean the destruction of the human race.' The strain was all the greater because the President had ordered that not a whisper of the crisis should get into the media (something that would be impossible today when satellite TV companies could discover the sites for themselves). Only a tightly knit group of men in the White House knew about the peril the world faced for those 13 days in October 1962.

The wall of secrecy was breached on the evening of Monday 22 October when John F. Kennedy went on television to address the American people. By now he had decided that a naval blockade of Cuba, which would stop more missiles and spare parts being sent, was by far the best option available. He told the American people that he was asking for an emergency meeting of the UN **Security Council** and called on Khrushchev to 'halt and eliminate this clandestine, reckless and provocative threat to world peace and to stable relations between our two nations'. Kennedy also told the American people that a naval blockade would be mounted around Cuba.

One hundred and eighty ships were now sent to blockade the island and intercept any Soviet ships that might be bringing missiles or spare parts. America's B-52 bomber force was also sent into the air loaded with atomic weapons. Robert Kennedy wrote in his book that 'We went to bed that night filled with concern and trepidation'.

INTERNATIONAL REACTION

John Kennedy was able to rely on his main allies in Europe for support. They were shown detailed photographs of the missile sites, although de Gaulle told the US Ambassador that he did not need to see them as 'a great government such as yours does not act without evidence'. Immediate support was forthcoming from West German Chancellor Konrad Adenaeur and Prime Minister Harold Macmillan.

Equally important for the Kennedy Administration was securing the support of America's Central and Latin American neighbours via the **Organization of American States** (OAS) Charter. Kennedy got unanimous support from the OAS for a blockade of Cuba. Not all foreign opinion was persuaded. The famous British philosopher, Bertrand Russell, sent the US President the following message. 'Your Action Desperate ... No Conceivable Justification. We Will Not Have This Mass Murder ... End This

KEYWORD

Organization of American States: the regional body representing American states on which the USA has the dominant role.

Madness.' Kennedy told him that this was a bit like attacking someone who had intercepted a burglar in their own house. Russell had sent a much more friendly message to Khrushchev.

On Thursday 25 October, there was outright confrontation between the United States and the USSR at the United Nations in New York. US Ambassador Adlai Stevenson (who had twice run unsuccessfully for the Presidency in 1952 and 1956), demanded that his Soviet counterpart give a reply to his question about whether the Soviet Union had put nuclear missiles into Cuba. When Ambassador Zorin declined to do so, Stevenson thundered, 'I am prepared to wait for my answer until hell freezes over. And I am also prepared to present the evidence in this room – now!' At this point, aerial photos were wheeled into the Security Council chamber, whereupon Zorin tried to deny their authenticity. But Stevenson's speech dealt a devastating blow to Soviet credibility in the eyes of world opinion.

EYEBALL TO EYEBALL

Nevertheless, work continued on the nuclear missile sites in Cuba, although the crisis was beginning to be defused. During the night of 24–25 October, six Soviet vessels carrying nuclear warheads and other equipment turned around and headed away from Cuba. Kennedy ordered US vessels to give any following Soviet ships the chance to do so too. Dean Rusk told a colleague, 'We're eyeball to eyeball, and I think the other fellow just blinked'. In fact, Khrushchev had decided that the USSR would not test the **quarantine** with ships carrying weapons. He had not ordered all ships to turn round.

KEYWORD

Quarantine: the other technical word used for the blockade of Cuba.

Secret contacts were now being made by Bobby Kennedy with a Soviet representative in Washington called Bulshakov (obviously with the President's full approval). Such channels allowed secret diplomacy to be pursued, but John Kennedy refused to celebrate about the turning back of the Soviet ships. He told aides, 'You don't want to celebrate in this game, this early'. He was right. The Russians could still make the missiles on Cuba operational. What was Khrushchev thinking in Moscow?

THE MESSAGES

This became clear in a lengthy letter which the Soviet leader sent to Kennedy at 9.30 US time on Friday 26 October. Khrushchev tried to pretend that the weapons shipment to Cuba was complete and that they were for defensive purposes only. He declared his commitment to peace but said this could be achieved only if the USA promised not to invade Cuba, and removed its quarantine. If this were done, there would be no need for the Russians to have a presence on Cuba. In New York, the Cuban delegation at the UN hinted that a guarantee about Cuba's integrity could mean that the missiles sites were dismantled. Arthur Schlesinger wrote later that 'The President probably had his first good night's sleep for ten days: certainly the rest of us did'.

The relief didn't last. Early on the Saturday morning (27 October), a much more aggressive message from Khrushchev came over Moscow Radio, demanding that Jupiter missiles be removed from Turkey before any concession could be made over Cuba. Then JFK got news that a U-2 had been shot down over Cuba. Kennedy refused to be pushed into a premature response.

The State Department had prepared a letter that rejected a swap of the Jupiter missiles for the Soviet ones on Cuba. But Robert Kennedy and Ted Sorenson talked the President out of sending it. Instead the second, aggressive Khrushchev letter was ignored and an answer was sent to the first more conciliatory one. This decision was reached only after intense debate in the Cabinet Room on the Saturday afternoon. His brother noted that among all the tired and anxious men there, 'President Kennedy was by far the calmest'. The President decided not to make a military response to the Russian shooting down of the U-2 spy plane. And he told Khrushchev that he had read his letter of 26 October 'with great care and welcomed the statement of your desire to seek a prompt solution'. Kennedy noted Khrushchev's desire for peace, and said that if the Soviet leader wanted détente between the **Warsaw Pact** and NATO, he would be willing to discuss it. The message was duly sent off to Moscow. At the same time,

KEYWORD

The Warsaw Pact: the defence pact signed in 1955 between the USSR and its communist satellite states.

Robert Kennedy took a copy to the Soviet Ambassador. The USSR was solemnly warned that if no assurances were received within 24 hours, the US would take military action on Tuesday 30 October.

The President ordered Ex-Comm to meet at 9 on Sunday morning. He and his colleagues waited for Khrushchev's reply in the watches of the night in unbearable tension. Sunday 28 October 1962 was a bright sunny day. At about 9 a.m., Khrushchev's reply came in and it was conciliatory. He would stop all work on the missile sites in Cuba and the missiles would be crated and returned to the USSR. Talks would start at the UN. It was clear therefore, in Arthur Schlesinger's words, that Khrushchev had 'thrown in his hand'.

It had been a very close call. Kennedy said shortly afterwards that 'If we had invaded Cuba … I am sure the Soviets would have acted. They would have to, just as we would have to'.

AFTERMATH
President Kennedy gave orders that there should be no triumphalism over the Cuban Missile Crisis. He went on television and referred merely to Khrushchev's 'statesmanlike decision'. In his crisis management he had undoubtedly been influenced by Barbara Tuchmann's *The Guns of August*, which chronicled the great power's slide into war in 1914, and which he had been reading at the time.

Yet there had been serious errors on the American side. One was the assumption that the USSR would never put missiles into Cuba, despite clear indications to the contrary. Another was the view taken by Kennedy and his brother that Castro's overthrow might be worth risking a nuclear war. Foreign observers criticized Kennedy, with some reason, for not seeing that Khrushchev had as good a case about missiles in Turkey as the President did about Cuba.

CONSEQUENCES
The Cuban missile crisis of October 1962 gave the two superpowers a severe fright. Never again in the protracted Cold War (which ended

with the collapse of the USSR in 1991) did Soviet Russia and the United States come so close to war.

Its immediate results were:

* Cuban sovereignty was respected and the US promised not to invade

* the Soviet missiles and personnel were removed

* some time later, with minimal publicity, the Jupiter missiles were removed from Turkey

* a **hot line** was installed between Moscow and Washington in case of future threats of war

* in 1963 the USA, USSR and Britain signed a Test Ban Treaty which outlawed testing nuclear bombs in the atmosphere.

KEYWORD

Hot line: the special telephone linking the US President and the Soviet Premier.

CONCLUSION

The accounts of the Missile Crisis produced by Robert Kennedy, and by Ted Sorenson and Arthur Schlesinger in the 1960s, portray President Kennedy as a hero. Given the closeness of these men to the President, this is unsurprising, but since the 1960s Kennedy's policy has been more critically appraised. Although he handled the crisis with coolness, he was in many respects an archetypal Cold War Warrior whose assumptions about Third World leaders like Castro were often inaccurate. Nevertheless, his willingness to give his opponent leeway in the Missile Crisis undoubtedly helped to save the world from nuclear war. Hawkish attitudes in the Pentagon could have led to catastrophe. The Missile Crisis had:

* strengthened Kennedy's authority as President

* made him aware of the need for closer communication links with Moscow in the event of a crisis

* opened his eyes to the dangers created by both superpowers having misperceptions about the other

* strengthened Robert Kennedy's position in the circle of JFK's closest advisers

Kennedy and the Vietnam War

John F. Kennedy inherited another major foreign policy issue from the Eisenhower administration apart from Cuba. This was the war in Vietnam which was starting to become a really serious problem by the time the President died in 1963. Admirers of Kennedy have suggested that had he lived, he would never have allowed a situation to develop whereby 500,000 US soldiers were to be in Vietnam in 1968. Oliver Stone's recent film biography even suggested (without any hard evidence) that it was precisely because Kennedy was about to withdraw from Vietnam that he was assassinated. Historians have continued to speculate on whether the catastrophe of 1975, when US personnel had to be airlifted off the roof of the US Embassy in Saigon to avoid capture by the communists, could have been avoided if Kennedy had lived.

THE BACKGROUND

Vietnam, together with Laos and Cambodia, had been part of the French Indo-Chinese empire until 1954. Following a decisive defeat at the hands of the **Vietminh** in that year, the French were forced to withdraw. Under the terms of the Geneva Agreement, Vietnam itself was divided along the seventeenth parallel, a geographical line of latitude. North of that line, the communist administration of **Ho Chi Minh** would hold sway, while south of it, a non-communist government would do so. But the accord also made provision for national elections to take place within two years of partition to reunify the country. This opened the real possibility that Ho Chi Minh and the Vietminh, a largely communist organization, would win such elections. Certainly the British who, with

KEYWORDS

Vietminh: an abbreviation of Vietnam Doc lap Dong minh meaning League for the Independence of Vietnam.

Ho Chi Minh: meaning 'He who enlightens'. Ho's real name was Nguyen Ai Quoe.

the Chinese, were Co-Chairmen of the Geneva Conference, expected the Vietminh to win national elections in Vietnam, a fact that they were prepared to accept. But the Americans were not. Eisenhower and his hawkish Secretary of State, John Foster Dulles, were unenthusiastic participants in the Conference.

US policy was based on the so-called domino theory which suggested that if one country in South East Asia, such as Vietnam, were allowed to go communist, the rest would follow like a row of dominoes. Thus Vietnam, and indeed all of former French Indo-China, had to be held against the communist Vietminh and their communist sister organizations in Laos and Cambodia (now Kampuchea).

KENNEDY AND VIETNAM

President Kennedy had taken an interest in Indo-China for many years. In the early 1950s, he had visited Vietnam during the French colonial war against the Vietminh. Jackie Kennedy had also translated large extracts from a book by the French writer, Paul Mus, on the French colonial war which had dragged on from 1946 to 1954. Kennedy himself became one of the organizers of the 'American Friends of Vietnam' organization that was set up in 1956. He said at the time that Vietnam represented 'the finger in the dyke' in the war against global communism. Kennedy was, and remained, a Cold War Warrior convinced that the line had to be held against the threat of Soviet and Chinese communism.

THE REGIME OF NGO DINH DIEM

American refusal to permit national elections in Vietnam allowed their choice as ruler, Ngo Dinh Diem, to prosper in South Vietnam. Diem came from the **mandarin** class in the North and was one of 600,000 northerners whom the Americans had encouraged to flee southwards

KEYWORD

Mandarin: meaning government official or civil servant. The Vietnamese copied the Chinese ruling system.

in the years after 1954. He was also a Catholic, and blatantly favoured his fellow Catholics, having also approached members of the American

Catholic community for support (such as Joseph P. Kennedy) when he was an exile in the United States in the early 1950s. Nepotism was another feature of Diem's regime. One brother was a government minister and another was Catholic Archbishop of the imperial city of Hué. His father-in-law became South Vietnamese Ambassador in Washington. This was the corrupt South Vietnamese regime that Kennedy inherited when he became President in 1961.

Diem was faced by a full-scale communist revolt in the South from the so-called **Viet Cong**, who were supported by Ho Chi Minh's regime in the North. He became increasingly autocratic in the Kennedy years, even throwing out NBC and CBS TV reporters, and banning

KEYWORD

Viet Cong: meaning People's Liberation Armed Forces.

the magazine *Newsweek* in South Vietnam for daring to criticize his policies.

THE AMERICANIZATION OF THE WAR

President Kennedy was well aware of the difficulties that an increased US commitment to South Vietnam might mean. He told a friend privately that 'We've got to face the fact that the odds are about a hundred to one that we are going to get our asses thrown out of Vietnam'. He was clearly sceptical about military advice that suggested that more arms and more men would solve the problem. Yet he seemed to lack the moral courage needed to pull out of Vietnam altogether, even though he was well aware of France's costly failure in the country in the years before 1954. Kennedy never really seems to have questioned the relevance of the domino theory, even though the United States had recently fought a war in Korea which had ended in a bloody stalemate.

What Kennedy did was to follow a middle course in Vietnam, a strategy that had worked well enough in the Cuban Missile Crisis when he had rejected the extreme military solutions put forward by the Pentagon. In Vietnam, the two radical options facing him were:

* a negotiated settlement with the communists

* escalation of US military involvement up to the figure of 200,000 troops some top advisers wanted.

Kennedy rejected both these options, but in 1961 he did permit an increase in both the number of US military advisers and the amount of military equipment sent to Saigon. Most of the fighting, however, was still left to the **ARVN**.

WAR IN THE COUNTRYSIDE

The problem facing the Americans was that they were teaching the ARVN the methods needed to fight a conventional army, when the Viet Cong and their North Vietnamese allies

> **KEYWORDS**
>
> ARVN: Army of the Republic of Vietnam (South Vietnam).
>
> Guerrilla: the Spanish word for soldier.

used **guerrilla** tactics that allowed them to disappear into the paddy fields, the jungle or the mountains of the South. These methods had already been tried unsuccessfully by the French whose forces had included very tough Foreign Legionnaires.

The Americans did recognize that the Diem government was losing the war in the countryside and that something had to be done to win over the millions of Vietnamese peasants. They therefore experimented with the idea of 'strategic hamlets' whereby villages were protected from Viet Cong incursions. By day, the peasants worked in the rice fields, they then returned to their villages under the protection of the soldiers. The problem was that at night the 'VC', as the Americans called them, would enter the villages when the ARVN soldiers were gone and intimidate the peasants. But this fact was ignored and Diem's brother Ngo Dinh Nhu, the Security Minister, made lavish claims of success which were passed back uncritically to Washington.

LBJ'S VISIT

John F. Kennedy never visited Vietnam while he was President. But in May 1961, he did send Vice-President Lyndon Johnson there. Johnson spent just 36 hours in Saigon and praised Diem as the 'Winston

Churchill of South-East Asia' (in highlighting the absurdity of this comment, Kennedy admirers such as Schlesinger overlooked the fact that on the way home LBJ, when asked why he had said this, replied 'Shit, Diem's the only boy we got out there'). Johnson admired Diem's qualities, if not those of his relatives, and recommended support for the regime but only if military and economic reforms were brought in. But Johnson was definitely not part of the Kennedy magic circle in Washington, so the President may not have been inclined to have taken much notice of what he said. Robert Kennedy had a low opinion of LBJ who soon became an enemy, but John Kennedy tried to soothe the Texan's notorious sensitivities by giving him something to do.

Nevertheless, the Johnson visit formed part of a pattern of fact-finding missions to South Vietnam, whose recommendations often contradicted one another. At home, there were hard-liners like McNamara at the Pentagon, who was an out and out supporter of the domino theory and wanted hundreds of thousands of US combat troops in Vietnam. And also liberals like Roger Hilsman, who wanted to avoid a large ground commitment and had a low opinion of Diem. Kennedy himself operated between these two extremes, worried about a big commitment on the ground, but unwilling to abandon Diem. It was, in the words of a journalist, 'all the way with Ngo Dinh Diem'. Other hard-liners like Walt Rostow (who went to Vietnam) thought the conflict was a dangerous **war of liberation** which had to be contained.

> **KEYWORD**
>
> War of Liberation: the phrase used by communist leaders like Krushchev to describe guerrilla campaigns against the West in Asia.

THE FALL OF DIEM

There was considerable dissatisfaction with the Diem government inside South Vietnam. He consistently favoured his relatives and fellow Catholics who received top jobs in government. He also consistently failed to carry through the reforms that the Americans had been promised. Worse still, Diem seemed prepared to deliberately alienate the Buddhists (80 per cent of the population), by interfering with their freedom of worship. It came as little surprise, therefore, when dissident ARVN officers tried unsuccessfully to overthrow Diem in 1960.

By 1963, this misguided policy was having serious consequences, and Kennedy was seriously having to review his administration's attitude towards the Diem government. In essence, Kennedy had three options. He could:

* continue to give Diem all-out support

* withdraw his support completely and secure Diem's removal, by force if need be

* secretly support a coup against Diem while publicly continuing to support him.

Effectively, Kennedy chose the last option while trying to preserve the illusion that he could stop a coup if he wished to. But he allowed the US Ambassador in Saigon, Henry Cabot Lodge (Kennedy wanted a Republican involved in case anything went wrong), to encourage rebel generals.

Meanwhile, Diem's persecution of the Buddhists continued and his brother's secret police broke into pagodas to make arrests. In July 1963, a 73-year-old Buddhist **bonze** burnt himself to death in full public view in Saigon in

KEYWORD

Bonze: meaning a Buddhist monk.

protest against Diem's policies. The response of Diem's hard-line sister-in-law, Madame Ngo Dinh Nhu, became notorious. She told CBS News that the Buddhists had just 'barbecued a bonze with imported gasoline' and that she would provide the mustard for any more barbecues. The Americans advised Diem to get this heartless woman out of the country but he would not listen. Kennedy himself was very shaken, remarking that 'no news picture in history has generated as much emotion around the world'. To this day, the car used to drive the monk,

Trich Quang Duc, to Saigon is kept on a Buddhist pagoda site at the imperial city of Hué.

From this point, the anti-Diem group in Washington became more and more influential. Led by the veteran Averill Harriman, it sent a cable to the Saigon Embassy which said that if Diem would not remove Nhu and his secret police apparatus, then the United States should withdraw its support. Kennedy saw the cable but did not object to its contents, thus effectively endorsing a coup against Diem. Those who supported Diem were furious about the lack of consultation and the resulting rows worried the Kennedy brothers. But by saying nothing, JFK made a coup virtually inevitable. Other comments were just ambiguous. He told Cabot Lodge, for example, in October that 'while we do not wish to stimulate a coup, we also do not wish to leave the impression that the US would thwart a change of government'. In fact, the anti-Diem generals in Saigon were not content with just removing Diem for on 2 November, they murdered both Diem brothers in cold blood.

Kennedy was shocked, but he had only himself to blame for he had overestimated his power to control the anti-Diem ARVN military in Saigon. His policy of trying to keep options open just did not work in the volatile atmosphere in Saigon in the summer and autumn of 1963. He could not know that within three weeks of the assassination of the Diem brothers, he himself would be dead.

VIETNAM: THE KENNEDY LEGACY

At the point when President Kennedy died, there were some 16,000 US military advisers in Vietnam. This was a small number when compared with the vast American commitment five years later. Historians have, therefore, focused on the issue of whether Kennedy would have pulled out of Vietnam much earlier than his successors Johnson and Nixon felt able to do.

Kennedy's admirers have argued that he would have been convinced by the logic of the US losses, which were running at 36,000 dead by 1968 and ultimately at 58,000. And the Kennedy family certainly encouraged the idea that JFK would have withdrawn. Some statements made by Kennedy at the time seem to encourage this belief as, for example, when he said in a TV interview in September 1963 that 'In the final analysis, it is their [the Vietnamese] war. They are the ones who have to win it'. The problem is that for every interview giving anti-escalation evidence, there is another providing the opposite. In that same month of September, for example, Kennedy told another interviewer that 'we should not withdraw'.

Kennedy's problem was his domestic context. Had he been re-elected in 1964 (as he surely would have been), he could not have been so, on a peace platform. Neither is there any real indication that US policy after 1964 would have changed direction. Leading figures in his administration, such as his brother and Robert McNamara, were hawks on the war (Bobby's anti-war conversion only came in 1967–68 when he had resigned from the Johnson administration), while much of US opinion still supported the war as late as 1968. Arguably also, Kennedy's prevailing interest in foreign policy would have stopped him becoming the effective domestic reformer that Johnson, with his vision of a 'Great Society', became. As far as the war itself was concerned, there was already evidence by 1963 that ARVN and their US advisers were fighting the wrong sort of war, but Kennedy was unable to prevent this.

In assessing whether Kennedy would really have put a stop to the Vietnam war, had he lived, we need to consider a number of factors:

* the extent to which JFK was a prisoner of existing Cold War preconceptions with their acceptance of the domino theory

* his unwillingness to face the sort of defeat the French had suffered

* his unwillingness to let down his South Vietnamese ally

* his tendency to underestimate the nationalist element in the appeal of Ho Chi Minh and the communists

＊ his problem as a Democratic president in being accused of being 'soft on communism' (the Party had been made the scapegoat for the loss of China to the communists in 1949).

When all these factors are considered together, they made the likelihood of a Kennedy withdrawal small. Everything about Kennedy's record on Cuba, on Berlin and on Vietnam shows him to have been a convinced Cold War Warrior. Not a reckless militarist (unlike Johnson's opponent in 1964, the Republican Goldwater), but a man who was certain that there was a global communist threat that had to be confronted. Oddly, for someone who knew something about history, John Kennedy seemed unaware of the sort of historic tensions that were to cause the USSR and China to fight each other in 1969, and Vietnam (by then unified under the communists despite the American effort) to fight a border war with China in 1978. The monolithic model of global communism in which Kennedy, his brother Robert, and Robert McNamara believed, never existed, as the latter was to admit ruefully many years later. Kennedy's convictions on Vietnam were honest enough, but his decision to escalate US involvement in 1961 was ultimately to prove catastrophic. The Vietnam of the twenty-first century is still communist (albeit in a much watered down form), and the domino theory proven to be misconceived (neighbouring Thailand is not). In the end, it is hard to disagree with the verdict of the American historian Diane Kunz, writing in 1997, that 'The former Communist world has lost its idols. It is now time for Americans to relinquish one of theirs'. On Vietnam, Kennedy was wrong. The irony was that where communism survived in Vietnam, which the Americans regarded as an errant child nation needing to be shown the error of its ways despite its ancient culture, it was to collapse in ruins in the USSR without a war ever having to be fought.

7 Crime and Sex

Throughout the twentieth century, the United States suffered a serious ongoing threat from organized crime. This was largely associated with the Mafia, a criminal organization with Sicilian origins, which rose to prominence in the 1920s. At the time, indeed, that J. Edgar Hoover became Director of the FBI. Yet throughout his period in office, Hoover affected to believe either that the Mafia did not exist at all, or represented a minimal threat. This was not the view taken by the Kennedy brothers who were particularly associated with a federal campaign against racketeering in the trade union movement. A major target was the **Teamsters** Union and its flamboyant leader, Jimmy Hoffa. Hoffa had known Mafia associations.

Both John Kennedy and his brother had some experience of the field of labour relations. As a Senator, JFK had been a member of the US Senate Select Committee on Improper Activities, otherwise known as the Rackets Committee, and in 1957 Bobby Kennedy had become counsel for the Committee. So began Bobby's crusade against Jimmy Hoffa which was unrelenting and carried over into his brother's Presidential term.

HOFFA AND THE KENNEDYS
John Kennedy was fascinated by Hoffa whom he recognized to be both intelligent and energetic. But he also fully supported his brother's campaign against Hoffa whose army of truck drivers was held together by graft, intimidation and fraud. But Hoffa had friends in the Republican Party who tried to protect him. In 1960, he had also campaigned for Kennedy's Democratic rival Humphrey (though

Humphrey had rejected the endorsement), in an attempt to keep the Kennedys out of the White House. Hoffa knew that if John Kennedy won, his union would be subject to further investigation and likely prosecution.

For Bobby, destroying Hoffa became as much of a crusade as getting rid of Castro had been. The same sort of rhetoric was used about 'getting Hoffa', and the younger Kennedy was so zealous in his anti-Hoffa campaign that doubts were expressed by legal experts about whether his behaviour as Attorney-General was constitutional. There is no suggestion, however, that at any point the President's support for the campaign run by his brother wavered. John Kennedy could be scathing about bleeding heart liberals whose theories were never tested outside campuses or Washington buildings. The world of Hoffa and his cronies was a seamy and violent one, but Hoffa represented a threat, hence Bobby's determination to get an **indictment** against him.

For his part, Hoffa was equally determined to 'do something about that son of a bitch Bobby Kennedy'. A Hoffa aide, who became a Justice Department mole, reported variously that Hoffa was planning to bomb the Attorney-General's house and was hiring a hit-man to shoot him. In the event nothing happened, but few doubted that Hoffa lacked the resolve to order such an assassination if he chose to do so. Ultimately, Bobby Kennedy was the victor. In 1964, Hoffa was sentenced to concurrent sentences for jury tampering and diverting union pension funds for his own use. By then, however, President Kennedy was dead.

> **KEYWORDS**
>
> Indictment: a formal charge which can bring a defendant into a court of law.
>
> Mobster: from 'the Mob', i.e. the Mafia.

THE WAR AGAINST ORGANIZED CRIME

The Kennedy campaign against organized crime was far more thorough than it had been under Eisenhower. Top **mobsters** such as Giancana and Marcello were arrested and put on trial, and this was but part of a wider effort. In 1960, only 88 mobsters had been indicted whereas for 1963, the figure was 288. This success made enemies for the Kennedys among the Mafia community, some of whose leaders were particularly infuriated because they had backed Kennedy in the 1960 presidential campaign. Threats against the two brothers were taken seriously after the President's assassination when the Mafia were among those suspected of orchestrating the killing. But it has to be said that no hard evidence linking the organization to the assassination has ever emerged.

KENNEDY AND THE MAFIA

What was extraordinary was that while his administration was waging war on organized crime, Kennedy was himself linked to the criminal organization. This was so for a number of reasons:

* Kennedy's mistress, Judith Campbell, was also the mistress of Mafia boss, Sam Giancana

* Campbell was also the mistress of mobster John Roselli

* Roselli in turn also had links with Frank Sinatra, a member of the Hollywood 'rat pack' which included the President's brother-in-law, the actor Peter Lawford.

As Attorney-General, Robert Kennedy (who also had a colourful sexual history) was alarmed by the President's philandering and tried to warn him off, without much success.

KENNEDY'S AFFAIRS

Reference has already been made to J. Edgar Hoover's knowledge of President Kennedy's extra marital affairs. John Kennedy shared his father's taste for sexual adventures and entry into the White House did little to restrain his sexual appetite.

The President used his brother-in-law, Peter Lawford, to make assignations with Hollywood stars such as Marilyn Monroe and Jayne Mansfield, but his amours were not restricted to Hollywood.

Secretaries, call girls and the wives of personal friends variously became Kennedy's mistresses and the perks of office were pressed into service in his affairs. **Airforce One** was used to seduce women, as was the White House swimming pool. Secret Service details were only too aware of the women who were being smuggled into, and out of, the White House when Mrs Kennedy was safely away. Jackie's compensation was to spend many thousands of dollars on clothes and jewelry or to make privately cutting comments about her husband's philandering.

KEYWORD

Airforce One: the personal aircraft of the President of the United States.

The President's affairs were common knowledge among press and TV reporters but they never became publicly known. It has been suggested that had they become so, Kennedy might have been defeated in the 1964 presidential election, but this must remain supposition. Kennedy was, however, careful to try to restrict his choice of mistresses to women who had no known links with the Republican Party. But had Judith Campbell Exner (as she became) gone public, as she did in 1997, with the accusation that she had been forced to have an abortion which the Kennedys paid for, even the glamorous Kennedy image might not have saved the President.

Why was Kennedy's sexual behaviour so reckless? There was clearly a genetic element, given Ambassador Kennedy's behaviour, which had encouraged John Kennedy to take mistresses as a young man. And wives in the 1950s and 1960s tolerated sexual behaviour in a way which they would be unlikely to do now.

It has also been suggested that medical treatment might have increased Kennedy's libido because he was being prescribed both amphetamines and steroids. The irony was that Jackie Kennedy was being prescribed the same medicines by an unorthodox White House doctor called Max Jacobson. Kennedy reportedly remarked that if he did not have a regular supply of women, he got bad headaches, but the real explanation for his excessive philandering seems to lie with the Kennedy ethos. Joe Kennedy had treated women as playthings and he brought up his sons to do the same. Rose Kennedy, as a devout Catholic, disapproved of her husband's unfaithfulness but turned a blind eye to it over the years. And it was Joe, rather than Rose, who was the dominant influence over the Kennedy children of both genders. Whether Joe and John Kennedy did indeed share the same mistress must remain a matter for speculation but there is no doubt that John, like his father, was a sexual predator.

Bobby Kennedy was more discreet about his affairs but he, too, has been linked with Marilyn Monroe and the film star Lee Remick. Edward Kennedy, by contrast, has been as careless as his older brother and his repeated affairs have been associated by biographers with his wife Joan's problems with alcohol.

It can be argued that as first citizen, Kennedy set a terrible example with his persistent sexual philandering. Yet he never seemed to show any deep remorse about it and continued to go to Mass regularly on Sundays. One can only wonder what the venerable Cardinal Cushing, a long-standing family friend, would have thought about the President's immorality had he known about it. Kennedy posed as the good Irish-American Catholic family man when in reality the truth was very different. He was extremely fortunate that those in the media who knew about his affairs (and not all did), kept quiet about them. In a later age, he would not have been so lucky, not because morals were stricter, but because the media was far more unscrupulous.

None of this is to say that Kennedy's sexuality interfered with his capacity to run the United States effectively. He was not a Warren G. Harding who reputedly spent most of his time in the White House gambling and drinking, or a Calvin Coolidge who spent much of his dozing in his rocking chair. Kennedy was a highly sexed man whose relationship with his wife, for whatever reason, didn't satisfy his sexual needs. But his political failings, just like his political talents, cannot convincingly be linked to his penchant for extra-marital sex. He can be charged with being a poor role model and with a degree of hypocrisy, but Kennedy the philanderer was the same man who probably prevented a global nuclear war from breaking out in October 1962.

Nevertheless, it can be said that had the knowledge of Kennedy's behaviour become publicly known, either before or shortly after his death, the myth of Camelot would have been destroyed at its genesis. The sanitized biographies of Kennedy produced by Schlesinger and Sorenson in 1965 made no reference to Kennedy's seamy private life, and this can hardly have been because those two close aides did not know about it (Sorenson had worked for Kennedy since 1953). So great was the prestige of the presidency in those days, and so great the mythology associated with the martyred President that it would have seemed like a form of treason to accuse the dead Kennedy of being a womanizer.

Different times, different customs. Kennedy's behaviour was reckless and unseemly. Yet he did not lack some awareness that his affairs were potentially disastrous. He showed great interest, for example, in questioning the then British Opposition Leader, Harold Wilson, about the notorious **Profumo Affair** when Wilson visited Washington in 1963. Wilson was reportedly

KEYWORD

Profumo Affair: triggered by accusations in 1963 that the British War Minister, John Profumo, had an affair with a call-girl.

amazed when a scheduled short conversation turned into a two-hour quiz about the affair which had undermined the authority of the Macmillan Government in London. Kennedy, therefore, sniffed danger, but would he have changed his habits had he lived? There is precious little convincing evidence that he would have done so. For, as one historian has written, 'Like father, like son; Jack's passions were about evenly divided between the chase for office and the chase for women'. Just as old Joe had slept with Gloria Swanson from Hollywood, Jack (J. F. Kennedy) slept with Marilyn Monroe. If this sounds like an indictment of the Kennedy years, it needs to be remembered that the President belonged to a family to which normal rules appeared not to apply. Just as one of the Kennedys was destined to be President, so society's rules, even when emphasized in a traditional Irish Catholic context, did not exist.

John F. Kennedy may have broken hearts and broken marriages, but the specialness of the Kennedys seemed to make him immune from any feelings of guilt. His brothers behaved in exactly the same way. But believers in nemesis may feel that the next generation of Kennedys was in some sense to pay for the sins of the fathers. At the time, under the shining surface of the Kennedy presidency, was a seedy underbelly that linked organized crime and sexual licence. This had little to do with the high-flown rhetoric of the Kennedy Inaugural in 1961 with its demands for sacrifice and renewal in America.

Mysteries remain. Was President Kennedy implicated in the mysterious 'suicide' of Marilyn Monroe in 1962, not long after she had publicly sung 'Happy Birthday' to him in the presence of Mrs Kennedy? Other versions appear to implicate Bobby Kennedy, also alleged to have been one of Monroe's lovers, but we may never know the answers to this question.

Some certainties do emerge, though, from any study of President Kennedy's private life:

* he was a man of relentless sexual appetites

* he could be reckless and indiscreet

* he was protected by a wall of media silence

* he made use of the privileges of office to procure women

* at no point did Kennedy show any guilt about his numerous affairs.

Some may argue that great men have great flaws. The answer to that perhaps is that Kennedy had not quite achieved greatness, but that his greatest flaw has now become public knowledge both inside the United States and outside it.

The Death of a President

John F. Kennedy had presentiments about his own death. He was also badly affected by the death of his baby son, Patrick Bouvier Kennedy, in August 1963. The child had survived for only 39 hours before dying of respiratory problems, and Kennedy had to be physically restrained from making a last grab at the baby's coffin by Cardinal Cushing, the Kennedy family's long-standing friend and spiritual adviser. Yet this family catastrophe seemed to have brought John and Jackie Kennedy closer together, according to close aides and family friends.

In other respects, the President's life seemed to be thriving in the autumn of 1963. His physical health in particular, an on-going problem throughout Kennedy's life, was better than it had been for some time. Steroids were effective in controlling his Addison's disease, and effective back treatment had been lessening the discomfort he had suffered since the war (the President had long been obliged to wear a supportive corset).

Kennedy was also enjoying family life. Caroline and John Jr were an increasingly important part of the President's routine and to the surprise of some, they were even allowed to play on the floor of the Oval Office while their father worked! Relations with Ambassador Kennedy also improved because of the compassion John Kennedy felt for his father after he suffered a stroke. The combative element in their relationship disappeared as the old man, much weakened by his stroke, spent his surviving years in a wheelchair.

As for his marriage, Jackie's complaints about his extra-marital efforts had been vigorous, and rumours had circulated about an alleged affair with the Hollywood actress, Marilyn Monroe. She committed suicide in mysterious circumstances in 1962, which later aroused suspicions about the involvement of others. But senior aides commented on a new closeness with his wife as the President belatedly realized the dangers associated with his reckless philandering. The mass media, of course, knew about Kennedy's affairs, but in a different era from today, it kept its knowledge to itself. The same was true about Vice-President Johnson who knew about Kennedy's extra-marital liaisons, just as Kennedy knew about his (FBI chief Hoover knew about both of them, of course).

On the political front, Kennedy was confident about re-election with a larger mandate in 1964. He expected the **Grand Old Party** candidate to be the extreme right-winger, Senator Barry Goldwater of Arizona (Nixon

KEYWORD

Grand Old Party (GOP): American political code for the Republican Party.

had disappeared from the scene temporarily after a humiliating defeat in the Californian governorship race in 1962). He was also thinking about possible changes in a second Kennedy administration. The veteran, Dean Rusk, was a candidate for retirement as Secretary of State with Bob McNamara at Defence his likely replacement. Bobby Kennedy was planning to leave the Justice Department in January 1964 to run his brother's re-election campaign. But would he want to carry on as Attorney-General thereafter? Even more urgent was the question of whether Johnson should be retained as the Vice-Presidential candidate in 1964. Bobby Kennedy wanted to 'dump' Johnson and find another candidate. President Kennedy was not inclined to do so, according to close aides, realizing that to defeat the Southerner Goldwater, he would need Johnson's influence in, and knowledge of, the Southern states. It was the North/South balance between JFK and LBJ after all which had secured the 1960 victory. Bobby Kennedy's prejudice against Johnson was apparently based on remarks the Vice-President was supposed to have made about Joseph P. Kennedy's appeasing tendencies in the 1930s. Johnson denied making the comments, but the allegation was enough to prejudice the ultra-loyal Bobby against him permanently. The President, as has been seen, felt some sympathy for Johnson, describing the Vice-Presidency as 'a horse-shit job'.

DALLAS

John Kennedy held his first strategy meeting for
his 1964 re-election campaign in early
November 1963. On 20 November, he and
Jackie attended a celebration party for Bobby's
thirty-eighth birthday at **Hickory Hill**. The
next morning, the President and Mrs Kennedy
flew to Lyndon Johnson's home state of Texas.

KEYWORDS

Hickory Hill: Robert
Kennedy's home in
McLean, Virginia.

Love Field: the local
Dallas airfield in 1963.

The aim of the trip, which included visits to San Antonio, Houston,
Fort Worth, Dallas and Austin, was both to garner votes and sort out a
local feud in the Democratic Party. For Governor John Connelly of
Texas, a firm Johnson supporter, loathed Senator Ralph Yarborough
and the feeling was mutual. Yet it was a mission undertaken at some
risk. The Kennedys were associated with civil rights in the South and
were hated for it. Posters had appeared in Dallas that showed
photographs of President Kennedy and the caption 'Wanted for
Treason'. A month before the Kennedy visit, Adlai Stevenson had visited
the city and been spat on in the street by a woman. A placard was also
used to hit the UN representative's head, and Stevenson privately
warned that a visit by John Kennedy might be dangerous. The febrile
atmosphere of hatred in Dallas and other parts of Texas in the autumn
of 1963 has been memorably described in Hans Habe's *Anatomy of
Hatred*, which was published shortly afterwards.

Nevertheless, the visit went ahead as arranged and seemed to be going
well. On the morning of Friday 22 November 1963 in Fort Worth,
Kennedy read a leading article which accused him and his brother of
being 'soft on communists'. The President was not unduly put out.
Addressing Fort Worth citizens in front of a local hotel, Kennedy
quipped that 'Mrs Kennedy is organizing herself. It takes longer, but of
course, she looks better than we do when she does it'.

Shortly afterwards, the President and his wife flew to Dallas. On arrival
at **Love Field**, the presidential party, accompanied by Governor
Connelly and Senator Yarborough, got into two cars for the journey

into downtown Dallas. They were open-topped with members of the presidential security detail taking it in turn to stand on the outside of the vehicles as the cars pushed through the crowded streets. The President commented on the friendly attitude of the crowds, and his car turned into Elm Street and past the Texas Book Depository building. Then, wrote Arthur Schlesinger later, shots rang out:

> faint and frightening, suddenly distinct over the roar of the motorcade, and the quizzical look on the President's face before he pitched over, and Jacqueline crying, 'Oh, no, no … Oh my God, they have shot my husband,' and the horror, the vacancy.

What followed was pandemonium. Secret Service Agents threw themselves over the Vice-President (in the second car) to protect him and both cars then roared off to the Parkland Memorial Hospital. Jacqueline Kennedy, her dress stained with her husband's blood, cradled his head in her lap. The President was operated on immediately but a bullet had caused catastrophic damage to his head, and it soon became clear that he was unlikely to survive.

Meanwhile, Robert Kennedy was at home at Hickory Hill. At 1.43 p.m. he received a telephone call from J. Edgar Hoover to say that his brother had been seriously wounded. The Attorney-General spent half an hour on the line to Dallas talking among others to a member of the Secret Service detail. Half an hour later, he

KEYWORD

Justice Department: the US government department that controls the FBI and the legal system.

came downstairs to tell **Justice Department** colleagues, 'He's dead'.

Shortly afterwards, Lyndon Baines Johnson was sworn in as the thirty-sixth President of the United States. Beside him, in Airforce One, was the wife of the dead President, still in her blood-stained pink dress. John F. Kennedy had served less than three years of his first Presidential term before he was slain.

The impact of the presidential assassination was devastating, both inside the United States and outside. At Harvard, where Kennedy had been a student and where he dreamt of working on retirement from the presidency, a student slammed his fist again and again into a tree. Norman Mailer, the author of the famous US novel *The Naked and The Dead* said, 'For a time, we felt the country was ours, now it's theirs again'. Arthur Schlesinger, who had worked so closely with the dead man, told a friend 'We'll never be young again'. British Prime Minister, Harold Macmillan, a particular friend of Kennedy's, spoke of how the President had somehow embodied 'all the hopes and aspirations of this new world'. Days later, the thirty-fifth President was buried at Arlington Cemetery with all the solemnity that the stricken American Republic could muster. Few who were alive at the time will forget the poignant moment when Kennedy's tiny son, not of course fully aware of what was happening, saluted his father's funeral procession.

AFTERMATH

Grief in the United States was mixed with bewilderment and fear. An assassin, Lee Harvey Oswald, was rapidly arrested, but within days he himself had been shot dead by a local night-club owner called Jack Ruby. All sorts of wild conspiracy theories began to circulate (and continue to do so). Among them were:

* the belief that somehow the Soviet Union was involved

* the suspicion that Castro was exacting some form of revenge

* that the Mafia, whom Bobby Kennedy had been investigating, were involved

* that disillusioned anti-Castro Cuban exiles were implicated.

Common to all these assumptions was the belief that Oswald, who only had a defective Italian rifle that he had ordered through a mail order company, could not have fired all the shots from the Texas School Depository building where he had been working at the time.

And despite the fact that it soon became evident that neither Soviet Russia nor Cuba were involved, conspiracy theories continued to abound.

President Johnson set up an official commission of inquiry under the United States Chief Justice, Earl Warren. It reported to Johnson in the autumn of 1964 offering a conclusion that both Oswald and Ruby had acted alone. But many remained unconvinced. In 1979, **The House** Select Committee on

> **KEYWORD**
>
> The House: an abbreviation commonly used in the USA for the House of Representatives.

Assassinations decided that it was likely that there was a 'second gunman'. And in 1997, ex-President Gerald Ford, who had been a member of the Warren Commission, admitted that when he was President (1974–77), he had suppressed CIA and FBI reports that Kennedy had been caught in cross-fire in Dallas. This evidence also pointed at the Mafia, supposedly resentful about Bobby Kennedy's drive against organized crime, after it had contributed funds to the 1960 election victory. Robert Kennedy seems to have had doubts about the circumstances of his brother's death but he never went public about them. He and Mrs Kennedy also appear to have interfered in the autopsy process, seemingly to prevent the knowledge of John Kennedy's Addison's disease from becoming public.

THE KENNEDY LEGACY

Why did John Kennedy's death have the overwhelming impact that it did? Over the years, historians and biographers have put forward several suggestions which focused on:

* Kennedy's youth, a President cut off in his prime

* martyrdom, with the idea that Kennedy was the victim of dark forces inside the USA

* potential lost with the idea that things (as in Vietnam) would have been managed quite differently had Kennedy lived

❋ the inherent violence and extremism in 1960s' America of which Kennedy was a victim.

It is certainly true that Kennedy's death left an immense vacuum at the time. He was young, charismatic and attractive. In this sense, he and his family contrasted sharply with both his predecessors and his peers in other countries. Khrushchev, Mao, Macmillan and de Gaulle were, after all, old men. Neither did their wives have the public appeal that Jacqueline Kennedy had, an asset of which her husband made full use. Kennedy also epitomized the new in a grim Cold War world, even if his foreign policy was in most respects quite traditional. He was also fortunate in that his legacy was initially guarded by skilful historians and biographers such as Arthur Schlesinger Jr and Ted Sorenson.

But with the passage of the years, Kennedy's reputation has taken something of a battering. His sexual peccadilloes in particular, in an age less tolerant of the Kennedy's careless attitudes toward women, have left a tawdry impression. That is not to say that political leaders who indulge in sexual licence are ineffective ones, rather that in a media-driven United States such conduct is now subjected to a merciless scrutiny. Had, for example, the Marilyn Monroe affair been reported on in the 1990s, it is likely that John Kennedy's personal morality would have become a very serious national issue.

More criticism has also been levied, as we have seen, at Kennedy's Vietnam policy and at his attitude towards black civil rights. In the latter case, it can be convincingly argued that Kennedy was in part constrained by a weak position in the Congress, but it is also true that he was not quite the great liberal that his admirers described in the decade after his assassination. As far as Vietnam is concerned, it has become increasingly difficult to distance President Kennedy from the débâcle and defeat of 1975. There is little in Kennedy's record that convincingly suggests that he would have abandoned the Vietnam adventure by the time a second Kennedy administration was due to end in 1969. On the credit side, however, is Kennedy's maturity and good sense in managing the Cuban Missile Crisis, even if its genesis owed much to a willingness to swallow Cold War norms. He also showed prescience in, for example, encouraging the process of integration in Western Europe. And when he was able to move away from Cold War constraints, Kennedy showed himself to be sympathetic to Third World problems.

The very manner and timing of Kennedy's death had its impact on his successor, Lyndon Johnson, who always felt himself to be the heir of Kennedy's policies. This was certainly true of Vietnam, although LBJ certainly proved to be gullible about the misleading military information he was being passed. And Johnson's landslide victory in 1964 allowed him to become a greater domestic reformer than JFK would probably have been had he lived.

THE KENNEDY CURSE

No leading family in recent history has seemed to live under such an unlucky star as the Kennedy family. This ill fortune had already manifested itself long before John Kennedy died in 1963, for Joe Kennedy Jr died in the war in a plane crash, and Jack Kennedy's favourite sister, Kathleen, or 'Kick' as she was known in the family, also died in a plane crash in 1948.

The pattern of premature death in the family did not end with the President's assassination, as is well known. Bobby Kennedy was traumatized by his brother's death, ill at ease in the Johnson administration and ultimately a critic of it. In 1968, he decided to stand against Lyndon Johnson in the Democratic primaries, and seemed to have every chance of getting the Democratic Party nomination. In early June, he won the California primary and made a brief celebratory speech at the Ambassador Hotel in Los Angeles. After he had done so, Robert Kennedy took a short cut through the hotel kitchen to avoid the crush of press and onlookers. As he did so, he was shot and killed by Sirhan Sirhan, a young Palestinian Arab who was aggrieved about America's pro-Israeli policy in the Middle East, and wanted to make a protest against it by killing Kennedy. Desperate attempts were made by a medical team to save Bobby who lingered for 25 and a half hours. But at 1.44 a.m. on Thursday, 6 June 1968, Robert Francis Kennedy was pronounced dead. He was just 42 years old, four years younger than Jack Kennedy had been when the assassin's bullet had claimed him. But just as had been the case with his elder brother, rumour suggested that Bobby too had been the victim of some sort of conspiracy. But it was Sirhan Sirhan who remained the official murderer, condemned soon afterwards to life imprisonment at Soledad Prison in California.

The dreadful symmetry between the brothers' deaths seemed to taint everything about the Kennedy family thereafter. Jackie Kennedy had already caused some controversy by marrying the Greek shipping magnate, Aristotle Onassis, regarded by many as a man of somewhat dubious character, who was very wealthy. Somehow it was not what Americans expected of an ex-First Lady, particularly in the full afterglow of the Kennedy myth.

Then it was the turn of the youngest Kennedy brother, Teddy, to attract unfavourable publicity. He had already been the subject of controversy when he was caught cheating in a Spanish exam at Harvard, but this was a trivial matter when compared with the notorious Chappaquiddick incident in July 1969 which resulted in the drowning of a young woman called Mary Jo Kopechne. Teddy claimed that he had driven his car off a bridge with Kopechne in it, but he failed to report the incident to the police immediately, thus arousing suspicion. Only the next day when the body had been found was he prepared to report to the police. It is almost certainly the case that Chappaquiddick cost Edward Kennedy any chance he ever had of becoming President (he ran against Jimmy Carter in 1980), although he served as Senator for Massachusetts for many years thereafter.

Seamy scandal continued to be associated with the family in the years that followed. Two of Bobby's sons, Robert Jr and David, had drug problems and David was to die of a drugs overdose in a Palm Beach hotel in 1983. A Kennedy nephew, William Kennedy Smith, was tarnished by a rape charge (he was eventually acquitted) and ultimately the family link with premature death reasserted itself when Joseph Patrick II crashed his light aircraft killing himself and his passengers in 2000.

Of all the Kennedy offspring, John Kennedy's own children Caroline and John Jr proved to be the most stable. John Jr went into journalism while Caroline was a happily married publisher. But otherwise the story of tragedy went on. In 1997, for example, Robert Kennedy's son Michael died in a skiing accident aged 31. By contrast, Robert's four daughters have been far more successful both in terms of career and longevity.

The story of the male Kennedys, however, has suggested that the celebrity associated with the two assassinated brothers became too much for the younger generation to bear. Rose Fitzgerald, by contrast, who lived to be 100, stood for the old Boston Irish Catholic virtues that had founded the Kennedy fortunes. But she lacked the rapport that Ambassador Kennedy had with the younger family members, and his authority. As it was, Joseph P. Kennedy, bedridden because of his stroke and unable to speak, could only be a silent witness to the tragic deaths of two more of his sons. He died in 1969. Whether he might, in better health, have been an influence for stability must remain a matter for speculation. Certainly Ted Kennedy with a serious drink problem has been unable to play this role. Bobby Kennedy's biographers have suggested that Ted Kennedy has been a poor influence on his eldest son Joseph.

The Kennedy story has been an extraordinary one. Joseph P. Kennedy was determined that one of his boys would be President of the United States and he achieved his ambition. Joe Kennedy Jr was earmarked for the role that was ultimately to be played by John, but there the would-be presidential dynasty ended. The Kennedys became American royalty in their time, and of them, John was the brightest and the best. It was his tragedy to be cut short in a political career which seemed to stand for a new generation in America. Over the years the Kennedy image has been tarnished, but in its day, the Kennedy Presidency did briefly seem to stand for new promise and new achievement. Whether John Kennedy would ever have become one of the truly great American Presidents must remain a matter for speculation. He has certainly been the most charismatic.

GLOSSARY

Airforce One The personal aircraft of the President of the United States.

Appeasement Meaning a policy of trying to reach an accommodation with another state. In the 1930s successive British governments were accused by critics of condoning German aggression by carrying appeasement too far. Appeasement became a dirty word in the USA after 1945.

ARVN Army of the Republic of Vietnam (South Vietnam).

Attorney-General The leading law officer in the USA. Unlike in the British system, the US Attorney-General has no seat in the Congress.

Bay of Pigs or the Cochinas Bay The site chosen for Kennedy's ill-fated invasion of Cuba in 1961.

Bonze Meaning a Buddhist monk.

Bug The colloquial expression for wire taps. The placing of such taps on someone's telephone.

Camelot The court of the legendary King Arthur. The term was used in the USA to sum up the romantic, youthful promise of the Kennedy Presidency.

Central Intelligence Agency The US governmental agency responsible for espionage abroad. Its headquarters is in Langley, Virginia.

Checkpoint Charlie The most famous crossing point between East and West Berlin before the Wall came down in 1990.

Cold War Warrior The phrase used to note those who were strongly hostile to the USSR and communism.

Congress The US Congress or parliament consists of two elected chambers. The lower house is the House of Representatives, and the upper house is the Senate. The US President, unlike the British prime minister, is not a member of the law-making body.

Covert Meaning secret. Carried out without public or Congressional knowledge.

District of Columbia The small area including the federal capital Washington which is not part of any US state.

Dixiecrat The name used for Southern conservative Democrats in Congress. 'Dixie' is a name for the old South.

Domino theory The American belief that the states of South-East Asia were like a row of dominoes. If one communist went, they all would.

Electoral College In the US electoral systems, there are effectively two elections. One is for the popular vote and the candidate who gets the most votes wins. But the second is the Electoral College, each state having a number of votes according to size. It is possible (as in 2000) for a candidate to win the most votes and lose the election, because a winning candidate *must* win the Electoral College.

Emigré From the French, meaning an exile from one's country.

Executive action Action taken by the President alone without reference to the Congress.

FDR (Franklin Delano Roosevelt) Roosevelt was often known by his initials, FDR, just as Kennedy was commonly referred to as JFK.

Federal Bureau of Investigation The FBI was created to prevent criminals escaping across state lines and so evading justice. Certain crimes (like kidnapping) became federal crimes and were dealt with by FBI agents.

Filibuster A tactic used in the Congress whereby a series of speakers deliberately waste time to stop legislation being passed.

The Foreign Relations Committee The Foreign Relations Committee of the US Senate (the upper house of the US Congress) has an important monitoring role where US foreign policy is concerned.

Freedom riders Young activists who challenged segregation in restaurants, waiting rooms and bus depots.

Gandhi The leader of the Indian independence movement was Mahatma Gandhi who advocated non-violence.

Grand Old Party (GOP) American political code for the Republican Party.

Guerrilla The Spanish word for soldier.

Hickory Hill Robert Kennedy's home in McLean, Virginia.

Ho Chi Minh Meaning 'He who enlightens'. Ho's real name was Nguyen Ai Quoe.

Hot line The special telephone linking the US President and the Soviet Premier.

The House An abbreviation commonly used in the USA for the House of Representatives.

Inauguration The process by which a new President comes into office, and is sworn in by the US Chief Justice.

Incumbent The word used to describe someone who is currently President of the United States.

Indictment A formal charge which can bring a defendant into a court of law.

Justice Department The US government department that controls the FBI and the legal system.

Lame duck An American phrase to describe the period between November and January, when the old president is serving out his time before the new president takes over.

Love Field The local Dallas airfield in 1963.

Mafia The shadowy criminal organization that originated in Sicily and was exported to the USA.

Mandarin Meaning government official or civil servant. The Vietnamese copied the Chinese ruling system.

Mobster From 'the Mob', i.e. the Mafia.

Monroe Doctrine In 1823, President James Monroe declared that any intervention by non-American states in either North or South America would be deemed a hostile act by Wasington, which could result in war.

The Movement of the Twenty Sixth of July Castro's rebel movement took its name from the unsuccessful attack by them on the Moncada barracks at Santiago in July 1953.

National Guard A part-time militia in the American states used to deal with civil emergencies.

National Security Council The specialist defence policy body which advises the President.

New Frontier In his acceptance speech at the Democratic Convention in July 1960, Kennedy spoke of a 'New Frontier' where the United States could fulfil its destiny by removing 'all forms of human poverty.'

Nomination In the US electoral system, Republican and Democratic contenders have to be nominated by their parties at a convention normally in July or August. Each US state has a number of votes at the convention, and sends a delegation to it. The candidate with the largest vote at the convention becomes the presidential candidate in the November election.

Nullification The supposed right of state officials to prevent any outside body, e.g. the federal government, from usurping power in the State.

Operation Mongoose The codename for the US plan to destroy Castro and his regime.

Organization of American States The regional body representing American states on which the USA has the dominant role.

Oval Office The office of the President of the United States in the White House.

Profumo Affair Triggered by accusations in 1963 that the British War Minister, John Profumo, had an affair with a call-girl.

Prohibition In 1919 the US Congress accepted the 18th amendment to the Constitution which prevented the manufacture, sale or transportation of alcoholic beverages. Prohibition, as it was called, was a disaster. Vast fortunes were made through illegal sales of alcohol, and in 1933 Prohibition was repealed.

Quarantine The other technical word used for the blockade of Cuba.

Republicans and Democrats By the 1930s the Republicans had emerged as the party of big business and the rich. Roosevelt (President 1933–45) created a Democratic coalition of trade unionists, blacks, Irish and Jewish Americans and the poorer classes.

SAMs Surface-to-air anti-aircraft missiles. Used to defend missile sites.

Secretary of State Shorthand for the Secretary of State for Foreign Affairs. Usually seen as a key post in the US administration.

Security Council The UN body which represents the great powers, allowing them to take emergency action when appropriate.

Summit So-called 'summit diplomacy' involving meetings between US and Soviet leaders was a feature of the 1950s and 1960s.

The Supreme Court The highest court in the US is the Supreme Court which can rule on whether or not actions by states or individuals breach the US Constitution.

Teamsters The International Brotherhood of Teamsters. A union for US truck drivers founded in 1903.

Transition The process by which the new US administration appoints key staff to replace those of the outgoing president between November and January.

TV debate The 1960 election was pioneering in allowing the rival candidates to be seen in debate against one another. When Nixon stood again in 1968, he would not agree to further debates. They could still be decisive as, for example, in 1980 when Reagan beat Carter.

U-2 The US intelligence spy plane.

Viet Cong Meaning People's Liberation Armed Forces.

Vietminh An abbreviation of Vietnam Doc lap Dong minh meaning League for the Independence of Vietnam.

War of Liberation The phrase used by communist leaders like Khrushchev to describe guerrilla campaigns against the West in Asia.

The Warsaw Pact The defence pact signed in 1955 between the USSR and its communist satellite states.

White backlash A term used in the 1960s to suggest that whites might react against civil rights reform.

White House The name of the President's mansion comes down to us from the Anglo–American war of 1812. The British burned the original building which was then repainted white to cover the burn damage.

Chronology of Important Dates

1917	John Fitzgerald Kennedy born in Boston, Massachusetts on 29 May.
1941–5	Kennedy's naval service in the Pacific.
1946	Kennedy elected as Congressman for Massachusetts.
1952	Kennedy elected Senator.
1953	Marries Jacqueline Bouvier.
1956	Kennedy wins Democratic Vice-Presidential nomination but he and Adlai Stevenson are defeated.
1960	Nominated as Democratic Candidate for the Presidency. Defeats Richard Nixon in election.
1961	Bay of Pigs Fiasco; Berlin Wall Crisis.
1962	Crisis over registration of James Meredith; Cuban Missile Crisis.
1963	Washington Civil Rights March; Assassination of Ngo Dinh Diem in Saigon; Assassination of John F. Kennedy (22nd November).
1968	Assassination of Robert Kennedy.
1969	Chappaquiddick Scandal.

FURTHER READING

Ambrose, S. (1989) *Nixon: The Triumph of A Politician 1962–72, Vol.2,* New York: Simon & Schuster

Beschloss, M. R. (1991) *Kennedy vs Khrushchev: The Crisis Years 1960–1963,* London and New York: Edward Burlingame

Collier, P & D. Horowitz, (1984) *The Kennedys. An American Drama,* New York: Summit Books

Gadney, R. (1983) *Kennedy,* New York: Holt, Rynehart & Winston

Gibson, B. & T. Schwartz, (1993) *The Kennedys: The Third Generation,* New York: Thunders Mouth

Halberstam, D. (1969) *The Brightest and the Best,* New York: Random House

Hamilton, N. (1992) *JFK: Reckless Youth,* London: Random House

Heymann, D. (1999) *RFK,* London: Arrow Books

Johnson, L. B. (1971) *The Vantage Point: Perspectives of the Presidency 1963–1969,* New York: Holt, Rynehart & Winston

Kennedy, J. F. (1969) *Why England Slept,* New York: Wilfred Funk

Kennedy, R. F. (1969) *Thirteen Days,* London: Pan MacMillan

Kunze, D. (1997) 'Camelot Continued' in N. Ferguson (ed.) *Virtual History,* London: Picador

McNamara, R. (1995) *In Retrospect: The Tragedies and Lessons of Vietnam,* New York: Times Books

McClear, M. (1981) *Vietnam. The Ten Thousand Day War,* London: Thames Menthuen

Manchester, W.(1963) *Death of A President,* New York: Harper & Row

Reeves, R. (1993) *President Kennedy. Profile in Power*, New York: Simon & Schuster

Schlesunger, A. (1965) *A Thousand Days: J. F. Kennedy and the White House*, London: Andre Deutsch

Sorenson, T. (1965) *Kennedy*, London: Hodder & Stoughton

Sorenson, T. (1993) *The Kennedy Legacy*, London: Mentor

White, T. H. (1961) *The Making of the President 1960*, New York: Athenaeum House

INDEX

CHURCHILL – A BEGINNER'S GUIDE

Nigel Rodgers

Churchill – A Beginner's Guide reveals the real Churchill behind the myth of one of the great figures in twentieth-century history. It follows the ups and downs of his often stormy career as soldier, writer and statesman. Learn how Churchill, a romantic and a rebel, fell out of favour many times before becoming Britain's greatest wartime leader in 1940. Churchill's defiant brilliance helped save Britain, and perhaps the world, from Nazi tyranny, to leave a near-mythical legacy.

Nigel Rodgers's fascinating text uncovers:

- the troubled childhood and youth of a rebel aristocrat
- Churchill's remarkable radicalism in a Liberal administration
- the wilderness years – Churchill is out of office but in the right about Hitler
- the hour of destiny – at last he becomes Prime Minister to rally the nation
- the legend – why the myth of the cigar-smoking great Englishman lives on.

CASTRO –
A BEGINNER'S GUIDE

Sean Connolly

Castro – A Beginner's Guide introduces you to the Cuban 'commander-in-chief' who since seizing power in 1959 has fashioned a communist society that has inspired international admiration and antagonized his superpower neighbour, the United States. Investigate how Castro outlasted contemporaries Khrushchev, Kennedy, Mao and Nixon in order to enter the new millennium as 'the last Cold Warrior'.

Sean Connolly's informative text explores:

- Castro's background and the times he lived in
- Castro's role in the Bay of Pigs and the Cuban Missile Crisis
- his friendship and rivalry with fellow revolutionary Che Guevara
- his contribution to revolutionary movements in Latin America and Africa
- how Castro has carried the Marxist torch after the fall of the Soviet Union.

GANDHI – A BEGINNER'S GUIDE

Genevieve Blais

Gandhi – A Beginner's Guide invites you to take a glimpse into the life of this profound character. Follow his extraordinary quest for morality, justice and spirituality and discover how his strategy of passive resistance achieved social reform.

Genevieve Blais's compelling text investigates:

- Gandhi's background and the times he lived in
- Britain's role in the history of India
- the events leading up to and prior to the Salt March
- Gandhi's role in the independence of India, his assassination and legacy.

LIVINGSTONE – A BEGINNER'S GUIDE

Peter Turner

Livingstone – A Beginner's Guide offers you a critical appraisal of the first man to bring an understanding of central Africa and its problems to the attention of the rest of the world.

Peter Turner's informative text explores:

- David Livingstone's background and the times he lived in

- his life as a missionary, doctor, explorer and opponent of the slave trade

- his remarkable friendship with H. M. Stanley

- his important scientific discoveries

- the ultimate effect of his work in relation to colonial development and African nationalism.